Devotionals for Bird Lovers

Under His Wings

Devotionals for Bird Lovers

Under His Wings

NANCY ROSE WISSINGER

A Division of WINEPRESS PUBLISHING

Pleasant Word (a division of WinePress Publishing, PO Box 428, Enumclaw, WA 98022) functions only as book publisher. As such, the ultimate design, content, editorial accuracy, and views expressed or implied in this work are those of the author.

Unless otherwise noted, all Scriptures are taken from the New American Standard Bible, © 1960, 1963, 1968, 1971, 1972, 1973, 1975, 1977 by The Lockman Foundation. Used by permission.

Scripture references marked KJV are taken from the King James Version of the Bible.

Scripture references marked TMB are taken from The Message Bible © 1993 by Eugene N. Peterson, NavPress, PO Box 35001, Colorado Springs, CO 80935, 4th printing in USA 1994. Published in association with the literary agency—Alive Comm. PO Box 49068, Colorado Springs, CO 80949. Used by permission.

Scripture references marked TLB are taken from The Living Bible, © 1971 owned by assignment by Illinois Regional Bank N.A. (as trustee). Used by permission of Tyndale House Publishers, Inc., Wheaton, Illinois 60189. All rights reserved.

Scripture references marked AMP are taken from The Amplified Bible, Old Testament, © 1965 and 1987 by The Zondervan Corporation, and from The Amplified New Testament, © 1954, 1958, 1987 by The Lockman Foundation. Used by permission.

"Something Told the Wild Geese." Reprinted with permission of Simon & Schuster Books for Young Readers, an imprint of Simon & Schuster Children's Publishing Division from POEMS by Rachel Field. Copyright 1934 Macmillan Publishing Company; copyright © 1962 Arthur S. Pederson.

Excerpt from "If You Find a Little Feather" in SOMETHING SPECIAL by Beatrice Schenk de Regniers. Copyright © 1958, 1986 by Beatrice Schenk de Regniers. Used by permission of Marian Reiner.

ISBN 13: 978-1-4141-0960-2
ISBN 10: 1-4141-0960-1
Library of Congress Catalog Card Number: 2007901118

Dedicated to my precious mother and daddy,
who built a loving Christian "nest" and maintained it for seventy-one years.

Table of Contents

Introduction

I grew up surrounded by cornfields in Central Illinois, and for as long as I can remember, my parents had birdfeeders in their backyard. I learned which birds we liked, and which ones we chased away! After I had married and moved away, my mother gave me a bird nest lined with her hair, which led to my collecting all types of bird nests. (I have since learned that it's against the law in some areas to take a bird's nest if there is any possibility that it might still be in use.) Most of my nests have been given to me by students (I taught elementary school for twenty-five years), and I always try to find one in the Christmas tree we cut in December. One of my favorite nests came from Bulgaria and is made almost entirely of feathers.

I am not an expert birder; in fact, I have never gone on any birding expeditions. I simply enjoy watching birds at my feeders, I subscribe to three magazines dealing with birds, and I frequently take bird books home from the library.

In the past few years I began thinking about the spiritual lessons to be learned from birds, and I started writing the devotionals in this book. I pray that you will read the suggested scripture portion each day; the devotional will be more meaningful to you. Whenever applicable, I urge that you respond to the plan at the end of each devotional by writing in a journal or using the blank pages at the back of the book. Writing things down will help you see what God is teaching you.

God's awesome powers are manifested in the world of nature – we marvel at majestic mountains, glorious sunsets, and powerful storms. *Under His Wings* shows us another dimension of God's creativity – the simple, yet amazing world of His feathered creatures. Most of us see birds daily but don't learn from them. Jesus told us to "consider the raven" – stop and take note of birds; they have something to teach us. This book encourages you to "consider the raven."

1
A Heavenly Nest

Read: Revelation 21:1-4, 18-24
Key verse: There will no longer be any mourning, or crying, or pain.

I have always been fascinated by bird nests. It never ceases to amaze me that a bird can construct one from mostly natural materials, using only its beak, body, and feet, and do it so quickly. Looking at the nesting materials tells us something about the bird as well as its geographical location. Birds typically use those supplies near their nesting spots – twigs, grass, leaves. Orioles use yarn and string, barn swallows use mud, and some birds weave nests of reeds. I have a hummingbird nest from Arizona made from desert plants; a Delaware hummingbird's nest would look quite different. No matter what a nest looks like, it's almost always lined with soft materials – hair, fur, feathers – that have instinctively been placed there to cushion the tender bodies of babies. Even the nests of eagles, made with large branches and rough sticks, are lined with seaweed or grass.

When I wonder what heaven will look like, I think about all the resources God used to create a perfect paradise. In the book of Revelation, the Apostle John tells us about gates of pearls, streets of gold, and precious stones in the foundations. Our minds cannot grasp the glory of our eternal home.

If the bird, one of God's simple creations, knows what kind of nest its young will need, how much more does the Creator of the universe understand what we look forward to in heaven? No death, no pain, no tears – and the joy of looking into the face of our Lord and Savior. Only God could create such a perfect "nest."

❖ Make a list of all the wonderful things we know about heaven.

Almighty God, thank You for preparing a place for us, that where You are, we may be also.

2
The Rooster's Pride

Read: Luke 18:9-14
Key verse: Everyone who exalts himself will be humbled.

With apologies to Jeff Foxworthy, you might be a city slicker if you've never heard a rooster crow on a summer morning. My kindergarteners enjoyed a little song that explained why the rooster sings: to wake up the farmer and the other animals. Actually, roosters see the morning light at least forty-five minutes before human beings do, and the feathered alarm clocks waste no time marking their territory. Like other male birds that begin singing at daylight, the rooster is saying, "This is *my* barnyard and these hens belong to me!" Scientists have discovered that a rooster recognizes the crowing of at least thirty other roosters. (Someone has said, "It's the rooster that does the crowing, but the hen delivers the goods.")

In an exquisite book of poetry called *Prayers from the Ark*, the rooster boasts, "Do not forget, Lord, it is I who make the sun rise." Sometimes we Christians are just as foolish. We wonder how God could manage without us, and we suppose that our churches would never recover if we took our talents elsewhere.

Even worse than the pride in what we *do* is the pride in what we *are*. Spiritual pride blinds us to our faults, and we become proud of our salvation. We forget how hopeless we are without Christ and how prone we are to sin. We can even become proud of our humility!

Proverbs 16:5 tells us that pride disgusts the Lord and leads to punishment. We need to continuously ask God to point out any pride in our thinking.

❖ Examine yourself – do you boast about how good you are, or about how great God is?

> *Father, I humbly admit that without Your help I can do nothing, and without Your grace, I __am__ nothing.*

3
Owling in Silence

Read: Psalm 46:1-11
Key verse: Be still and know that I am God.

In an award-winning picture book for children, a father and child go into the woods at night, hoping to see a great horned owl up close. The child knows "if you go owling, you have be to quiet." The only sound made is the father calling out the exact notes of the owl: "Whoo-whoo-who-who-who-whoooooo." If the owl is fooled into thinking another owl is present, it will fly close by to check. Sometimes the owling is successful, and sometimes it's not. There may not be an owl in the vicinity, or if there is one, it may not respond. One thing is for certain: if you're making noise, you won't hear the owl calling and you'll probably scare it away.

God tells us to be still, cease striving, or as *The Message* puts it, "Step out of the traffic." There are many things clamoring for our attention and time, and we have to stop now and then to home in on God's call. One bright note: our heavenly Father is always nearby and will respond when we call out to Him. He is available for a close encounter whenever we are. And we don't have to use any exact words – He hears all languages and can even interpret our sighs and groans.

We would need to turn off our cell phones to go owling, but we always have an open line to God.

❖ List a few ways how you could eliminate or minimize unnecessary interruptions in your daily activities.

> *Dear God, thank You for always being nearby and ready to hear me when I call. Help me learn to be quiet so that I can hear You.*

4
The "Lord God Bird"

Read: John 20:19-29

Key verse: Thomas answered and said to Him, "My Lord and my God!"

In April 2005, the news hit the birding world like a bombshell: the ivory-billed woodpecker was alive! Long thought to be extinct, this beautiful mysterious bird was photographed in Arkansas by a team of Cornell University scientists; conservationists joined bird lovers around the world in celebration.

One of the world's largest woodpeckers, it resembles the more common pileated woodpecker, but the ivory-billed has a wingspan of nearly three feet. The story is told that when people first saw the bird, they would say in awe, "Lord, God, what a woodpecker!" And thus the bird's nickname – the "Lord God Bird."

The news that Jesus was alive after His crucifixion was even more astounding and joyous. Two thousand years later people around the world are still celebrating, and will continue to do so throughout eternity. Christians will never be extinct, because Jesus is alive forever. The news of Jesus' resurrection didn't get the media hype of the ivory-billed woodpecker, but the event is recorded for all posterity in a Book that will also never be extinct. The dramatic exclamation of an awestruck Thomas will ring forever: "My Lord and my God."

❖ Listen to a recording of Handel's "Hallelujah Chorus" and exult in our Savior's resurrection.

Almighty God, I worship You with awe for allowing me to live with You forever in heaven.

(IVORY BILLED WOODPECKER)

5
Flight Path to Heaven

Read: John 14:1-12
Key verse: No one comes to the Father but by Me.

One way to recognize a bird is by the way it flies. Woodpeckers and gold-finches are recognized by their roller coaster flight, while ducks have a fast, straight flight pattern. Birds that fly infrequently and only for short distances are primarily gliders like pheasants and quail. Some birds, such as hawks and eagles, are soaring birds with large wings to catch the lifting forces of the wind. Many water birds depend on wind to become airborne, but some ducks, such as mallards, can jump right into the air. The speed of bird flight is also interesting. Songbirds usually fly about fifteen to twenty-five miles per hour, while falcons have been clocked at speeds as high as one hundred eighty miles per hour when diving after prey.

We Christians travel our spiritual path in many different ways as well. Some of us are slow and steady; other are on spiritual roller coasters. Many of us flap our wings almost constantly, while others seem to soar. We may "fly" in our own unique way, but the key truth is that we're all on the same flight path with heaven being our destination. Our arrival at that destination is only achieved by recognizing Jesus Christ as our Savior and trusting Him alone for salvation. While we may come to Him in a variety of methods and speeds, Jesus Himself said that He is the only way to God.

❖ Prepare to challenge the popular saying that all religions lead to God. Write down a few responses you might use.

Father, I want to be an effective flier, and move constantly closer to You.

6
Earthly Treasures

Read: Matthew 6:19-24
Key verse: Do not store up for yourselves treasures on earth.

One spring day many years ago my mother, with a towel around her shoulders, cut her thick brown hair. Then she shook the towel in the back yard. In the fall, Mother found a bird nest in the lilac bush near the barn. The tidy little nest was lined with her hair. She gave it to me, and I still treasure it, especially now that Mother has gone to be with the Lord. Some people would say the nest is worthless, but it is precious to me. I wouldn't trade it for an expensive work of art.

That nest was the first of many I have collected through the years. (It's important to be certain that a nest is no longer being used before taking it.) I enjoy displaying my nests in silk arrangements and fresh bouquets throughout my home. Several years ago, I was in the home of a woman who collected expensive crystal vases. When she asked me what *I* collected, I replied, "Real bird nests," and she wrinkled her nose ever so slightly.

Our most valued possessions are the things money can't buy. Our salvation is a free gift from God when we accept His Son as our Savior, and we even have mansions prepared for us in heaven. Some would say that their Bibles, lined with years of notes, are their most treasured possession. Our families, dear friends, good health, and precious memories are all gifts from God. And the gift of the indwelling Holy Spirit is priceless.

❖ Begin to fill a journal with a list of all your blessings that money can't buy.

Oh God, I am awed by how much You love me. My cup runs over with blessings. Thank You, most of all, for Jesus – my greatest treasure.

7
A Post of Safety

Read: Psalm 119:113-120
Key verse: Uphold me that I may be safe.

The literature of falconry contains many fascinating stories of hairbreadth escapes of birds from hawks or falcons. One story describes a magpie trapped on the open prairie by a hunting falcon. The magpie reached a barbed-wire fence post, and then proceeded to circle the post, always keeping the post between itself and the falcon. The magpie would not fly even when the trainer of the falcon walked up to it. Leaving the post would mean certain death.

One of the escape tactics of the skylark – one of nature's highest flyers – is trying to climb and remain above a high-flying falcon.

According to most bird observers, alert birds usually can escape attacking raptors (hunting birds). The key word here is *alert*. Not only do we human beings need to be alert to temptation, we need a "post" to keep between the enemy and ourselves. God has provided the post – Proverbs 18:10 says the name of the Lord is a strong tower; the righteous run into it and are safe. We can call on the name of the Lord anytime; a contemporary worship song says: "There is strength in the name of the Lord." Satan trembles at the name of the Lord; it reminds our enemy that he is already defeated.

❖ Start each day by calling on the name of the Lord – know where your "post" is.

> *Father, I praise Your powerful name. Thank You, Lord, for teaching me to call on You in times of trouble.*

(FALCON)

8
Identification Marks

Read: John 13:34-35
Key verse: By this all men will know that you are My disciples, if you have love for one another.

Serious bird watchers use a variety of methods to help them identify birds. Not only looking at the bird's shape, color, and size, but also paying attention to the beak (*bill* is the preferred term in bird watching) is important. Listening to its call or song is a clue, and observing the bird's habits, pattern of flying, and habitat tells a lot. Field marks – those specific features such as eye rings, wing bars, or breast stripes – help to narrow the possible birds that you are studying. Nests are often so unique that they pinpoint their maker – you can study the domed structure in your hanging basket and verify your suspicion that the bird darting in and out is a Carolina wren.

Jesus tells us that the world will identify us as Christians by our love. That one quality is difficult to fake. We can look and sing like Christians, but the extent of our love over a long period of time is really an identifying mark.

On the other hand, it is still important that our appearance, our speech, and our habits make observers curious if we are indeed Christians. We should stand out in ways that make people around us want to observe us closely to see the source of our loving, kind attitude. (And it helps if our "nests" are warm and inviting!)

❖ Look into your spiritual "mirror" to make sure others would identify you as a Christian. What are the clues?

Lord, help me to love others as You do.

9
Using Our Senses

Read: Acts 28:23-31

Key verse: And with their ears they scarcely hear, and they have closed their eyes.

The woodcock's chief source of food is the night crawler, so the bird must rely on its sensitive eyes, ears, and feet to find the worms. Because the ears of the woodcock are located close to its bill, they guide the bill in searching for worms. These ears detect the slightest movement beneath the surface and are the equivalent of being able to "see" underground.

The flexible end of the three-inch bill has many delicate nerve endings which feel the worm and signal the woodcock to pull it up. Even the woodcock's feet are sensitive to vibrations caused by the worm, and assist in locating its position. While the bird is feeding, its binocular vision gives a three-hundred-sixty-degree protection—the woodcock can see both ahead and behind.

In today's scripture reading, Paul is frustrated with his cantankerous Jewish audience. He reminds them that centuries earlier Isaiah had warned them about closing their senses to what God was saying. Paul sums it up by saying, "You've had your chance. The non-Jewish outsiders are next on the list. And believe me, they're going to receive it with open arms!" (TMB)

God shows us Himself when we open our ears and eyes to His truth and when we open our hearts to His Holy Spirit. Like the woodcock, we have the advantage of looking behind at what God has done and – through eyes of faith – looking forward to what He has promised in the future.

❖ Read Jeremiah 5:20-31 and compare this warning with Isaiah 6:9-10.

> *Father, I want to open all my senses to You so that I can receive all that You want to give me.*

10
Deadly Assumptions

Read: Proverbs 14:1-12
Key verse: There is a way which seems right to a man.

I have always assumed that the old phrase "thin as a rail" meant the narrow, shiny part of a railroad track. But I read recently about the marsh bird called a rail, and now I have a better understanding of what the phrase actually means.

Shy and secretive, rails are usually found in marshy vegetation. Their bodies are laterally compressed, allowing them to walk in dense grass or reeds. They can slide between stalks without disturbing the area around them, and their enemies are not aware of the bird's presence. Being "thin as a rail" is an asset that protects the bird.

Everyone makes assumptions. My assumption of the rail's meaning was innocent. But some assumptions can be dangerous or even deadly. Assuming that a gun is not loaded could be fatal, or assuming that the stranger at the door is friendly could have tragic results. Assuming that going to church makes one a Christian could have eternal consequences. The Bible does NOT say that doing good deeds or giving money to the church is the way to heaven; people making those assumptions are dead wrong. Jesus said He is the only way to eternal life – "no man comes to the Father but by me" (John 14:6). And Paul reminds us that we are saved by faith in Christ, not by doing good work (Eph. 2:8-9). Don't just assume you are going to heaven.

❖ Make sure you have trusted in Jesus to be your ticket to heaven.

Lord Jesus, I do believe You died for me, and I ask You to come into my life to be my personal Savior. I want to know for sure that I will spend eternity with You.

(RAIL)

11
Singing Like Larks

Read: 1 Peter 1:3-8

Key verse: Though you do not see Him now, but believe in Him, you greatly rejoice with joy inexpressible and full of glory.

Scientists can tell us a great deal about birds and their songs. We know birds sing to stake out their territory, and then when females arrive on the scene, the males sing to win a mate. During the nesting season, the male sings perhaps to please her, or to let her know he is near. Poets wonder how a bird feels when it sings, and how that song affects us human beings. Birds sing for many reasons – not just because they're happy – but certainly their songs can create a sense of joy and peace for us. The birds we heard early in our lives are the ones with the most power to stir our hearts – the birdsong of home has the most meaning for all of us.

One of my sweetest memories of growing up on the Illinois prairie is the song of the meadowlark, and I usually can hear one when I go home if I drive a back road with fences around the field. A group of larks is called an "exultation." Could it be that the birds are singing to praise God? Does God remind us every time we hear a bird that all nature exalts and worships the Creator? Should we not then be motivated to praise Him, too? We might not sing like larks, but we can surely use our voices to exult our God.

The next time you join voices with friends in church to sing, think of it as an "exultation of Christians."

❖ Sing a song to praise your Creator today.

Thank You, God, for a voice to sing and tell of Your majesty.

12
Colliding with Pride

Read: 1 Corinthians 10:12-15
Key verse: Let him who thinks he stands take heed that he does not fall.

One of the biggest dangers to birds is a window. Estimates suggest that over one hundred million songbirds are killed each year as a result of collisions with windows. The species most often involved are: American goldfinch, pine sisken, dark-eyed junco, Northern cardinal, mourning dove, and house finch. Most strikes happen during panic flights caused by the appearance of a predator. Experts suggest that one way to reduce bird collisions is to put decals on windows, especially near feeders.

What would you say is the biggest danger to Christians? Something almost transparent – perhaps so hard to detect that it needs a large "BE CAREFUL" decal? I suspect pride ranks very near the top. In fact, the busier we are doing the Lord's work, the easier it is to feel self-sufficient and proud of our "righteousness" – the very sin for which Jesus denounced the Pharisees and Sadducees. Perhaps we try to check ourselves spiritually by listing our good deeds, totaling the minutes we spend in church work, or seeing how many Bible studies we can finish in a year. Or we compare ourselves to other Christians and decide we're doing pretty well. And then we're stunned when we hit the window – the realization that we've become proud of ourselves.

❖ Check yourself for pride – examine your motives for your good deeds.

Search my heart, Holy Spirit, and show me how ugly my pride is. Do whatever it takes to make me humble.

13
Get Moving!

Read: Nehemiah 2:11–3:3
Key verse: So they put their hands to the good work.

The arctic tern leaves its nesting grounds in the Arctic Circle every fall and begins an eleven-thousand-mile journey to the opposite end of the earth. The tern covers approximately one hundred fifty miles a day and arrives in the Antarctic Ocean in time for spring. When it returns to the North Pole a few months later, it will have circled the globe in twenty weeks of flying. Determination is one reason the bird is able to achieve this seemingly impossible goal. Another reason is the task is broken down into smaller, achievable steps – the bird paces itself to fly one hundred fifty miles a day.

What is the lesson here for us? Determination is important, but having a plan is essential. If I want to break a bad habit, escape the cycle of depression, or recover from a heartbreaking divorce, I need to decide what steps to take – even if the first one is simply acknowledging I need help.

In today's scripture, Nehemiah had a goal – the daunting task of rebuilding Jerusalem's crumbling walls. He planned ahead, got good helpers, made up a schedule, and began working. It took Nehemiah and his crew fifty-two days to reach their goal. It takes the arctic tern ten weeks, and it may take even longer for us to achieve our goals. Ask yourself if it's worth it – then get moving!

❖ Read the first six chapters of Nehemiah.

Lord, give me a heart to work toward the goals You give me.

(ARCTIC TERN)

14
Finicky Purple Martins

Read: Hebrews 10:23-25
Key verse: Not forsaking our own assembling.

Purple martins are famous for being finicky when it comes to selecting a home. Many people have tried unsuccessfully for years to lure purple martins to specially-built nesting apartments. Bird books stress that *location* is the secret (haven't real estate agents been telling us that for years?). Martins require a large open area near water. The houses need to be fifteen feet high, and baffles should be used to keep predators from climbing the poles. You need to educate yourself about martins if you want them to make themselves at home in your yard.

There are a lot of people who are downright picky about choosing a church, and sometimes they waste time hunting for the "perfect spot." They complain that one church is unfriendly, another is too large, and yet another is too small. Some want a traditional service with lots of liturgy; other folks prefer a contemporary service.

Research indicates that when people are looking for a church home, they usually make up their minds before the service even starts. Location *might* be a factor, but it's more likely based on how friendly the people are. Choosing the right church for you and your family is important, but no church is perfect. Some people are never satisfied, and they have many excuses for not attending church.

Paul exhorts us to meet together regularly, and even though Jesus was sinless, he attended the synagogue every Sabbath. (Luke 4:16)

❖ If you haven't found a church home, start looking this Sunday! Decide in advance which things are essential and which things are preferable.

> *Oh God, lead me to a church that lifts up the Lord Jesus Christ, then help me discipline myself to attend regularly.*

15
Jealous Robins

Read: Exodus 20:1-4
Key verse: I, the Lord your God, am a jealous God.

In 1772, a naturalist wrote, "During the amorous season, such a jealousy prevails among male birds that they can scarcely bear to be together in the same hedge or field." More recently, scientists have concluded that this jealousy is directed more toward a plot of ground than mates. Robins are particularly famous for their territorial jealousy. They warn off rivals with angry cries; if an intruder persists, they dart out to attack. They may spend the better part of a day flailing at their own images in windows or hubcaps; they will repeatedly attack a fake bird.

In the winter, birds may share territories and food. But in the spring, the drive to have a safe place to raise their young leads the males to behave with energetic passion. The song sparrow, for example, will defend an acre or more, and some blackcapped chickadees patrol more than seventeen acres.

We tend to think of jealousy as an undesirable trait until we realize God is described as having a jealous love for us. He has a passion for defending His territory – the hearts of believers. He wants us to be completely His – no slight wanderings, no gazing longingly for things of the world, no other gods but Him and Him alone. God knows how easily we can be seduced, so He gave us the Holy Spirit to guard our hearts. We have His power to help us stay true to the Lover of our soul.

The robin attacking a fake bird isn't willing to take a chance; neither is God. He is prepared to fight for us.

❖ Look up "jealous" in the Bible's concordance; read the Old Testament entries.

Thank You, Lord, for Your divine jealousy – for wanting to keep me wholly Yours.

16
Hypocritical Wrens

Read: Luke 6:41-49

Key verse: You hypocrite, first take the log out of your own eye.

House wrens are adorable little birds, and people encourage them to live nearby in birdhouses. The male's loud, clear song is a favorite of many bird watchers. It's hard to believe such a little bird has such a big voice!

It's also hard to believe that this innocent-looking singer is guilty of deception and treachery. The male wren puts fake nests in several locations to convince other birds that the spot has been taken – "no vacancies." But even worse, the male deliberately pecks holes in the eggs of other birds to kill the babies. After watching this happen, many people choose to discourage wrens nesting nearby by removing the birdhouses.

It's disillusioning and disappointing when birds – or people we like – display ugly behaviors. It is especially disturbing when these people are church members. Jesus felt very strongly about hypocrisy and warned us many times to beware of guile and spiritual pretense. He also warns us not to judge others. So what do we do when someone's "walk" doesn't match their "talk"? We can pray for them, we can be careful not to gossip, and we can set an example by living discreet, upright lives. In today's reading, Jesus explains that each tree is known by its own fruit. What we do speaks louder than what we say or sing!

❖ Examine yourself – are any of your behaviors out of line with your Christian talk?

I want to be genuine, Lord. Please help me.

17
Birds Don't Worry

Read: Matthew 6:25-34
Key verse: So do not worry about tomorrow.

"Overheard in an Orchard"

Said the Robin to the Sparrow:
"I should really like to know
Why these anxious human beings
Rush about and worry so?"

Said the Sparrow to the Robin:
"Friend, I think that it must be
That they have no Heavenly Father
Such as cares for you and me."

(Someone has pointed out to me that this poem can be sung to the tune of "What a Friend We Have in Jesus.")

In today's scripture, Jesus tells His disciples not to worry about food or clothing. He points out that if God cares for the birds, He surely will care for us – He loves us and knows what we need, and we are far more precious to Him than birds.

In fact, the Bible says it is a sin to worry. The worrier is indicating that he doesn't trust God, or perhaps he thinks God isn't interested in our problems. *The Living Bible* says God will give you what you need "if you give Him first place in your life and live as He wants you to" (Matt. 6:33).

When we waste time and energy worrying, we aren't free to pursue the goals and challenges God has for us. We get so bogged down in what might happen tomorrow that we miss God's blessing for today.

❖ Write down your biggest worries. Isn't God big enough to handle them?

> *Father, forgive me for worrying. Remind me each day that You are able to do more than I even ask for.*

18
Shakespeare's Starlings

Read: 2 Samuel 12:7-14
Key verse: Because you treated God with such contempt...killing and murder will continually plague your family. (TMB)

In the 1890's, there were no starlings in America, but a group of Shakespeare fans thought we should know all of the birds he mentioned in his works. So they released sixty starlings in New York's Central Park.

Those sixty starlings started a great rolling flock that spread over the country, and by 1950 starlings had reached the Pacific Coast. They have done great harm to native birds and are a major reason for the decline of the eastern bluebird.

Sin wreaks even greater havoc in our lives. We think a "little" sin won't hurt us, but then it becomes a habit or a lifestyle. Families are destroyed, communities are weakened, and the moral fabric of society is affected. The Bible teaches that sins of one generation can extend into the future and become a curse on those who come after us.

Even though God forgave David the sins of adultery and murder, the consequences of the apparently simple act of watching Bathsheba bathe were terrible and far-reaching. "Little" sins have a way of mushrooming until they are out of control.

❖ When tempted to sin, consider the immediate and the long-term consequences.

Dear God, don't let me ever be nonchalant toward sin.

(STARLINGS)

19
Ways to Bathe

Read: Psalm 51:1-10

Key verse: Wash me and I shall be whiter than snow.

Most birds appear to enjoy bathing, which can be a communal activity with an entire flock participating, or it can be a solitary venture. The real purpose of the bath seems to be to thoroughly drench the skin and feathers. But birds have been observed going through all the motions of bathing in a dry circular container. "Air bathing" is a fairly common phenomenon that is touched off by the sight of other birds bathing in water. Many birds take dust baths – using their wings and feet to rotate in a dusty depression in the ground. Barnyard chickens bathe only in dust, never in water.

Sunbathing is another way the bird exposes its skin and feathers to an outside influence. Birds sunbathe much more in hot weather than in cool weather. It is not unusual for birds to fly from a bird bath to a sunny spot to sunbathe. Sometimes the water bath is followed by a dust bath. Birds will even bathe in snow. All of these practices promote healthy feathers and help the bird survive.

People need cleaning, too. All of us have sinned – we are dirty on the inside. There is no way we can get clean by ourselves – all of our good deeds are only surface remedies, and are even considered as filthy rags to God. Like birds, we may try various forms of cleaning ourselves. But we need the complete washing away of our sins that only Jesus can provide. In today's scripture, David pleads for a clean heart so he will be wholly pure from his sin.

John says in 1 John 1:7 that the blood of Jesus Christ cleanses us from all sin. Our hearts are cleansed only by faith in Him. Have you received His cleansing?

❖ When you bathe today, thank God for giving you a clean heart.

Father, wash me and I shall be whiter than snow.

20
Where Is Your Nest?

Read: Psalm 84:1-12
Key verse: The bird also has found a house.

Birds build their nests in a great variety of places – from window ledges in New York City to cliffs overlooking the Pacific Ocean. Nests are built in chimneys, in apron pockets on a clothesline, and on clumps of floating vegetation. I read of a pair of swallows that nested on a Tennessee River steamboat, and every day the swallows accompanied the boat in order to feed their young.

In today's reading, the psalmist envies the birds that nest near the altar of God in His temple and enjoy his presence. An old hymn says, "There is a place of quiet rest, near to the heart of God." Those of us who long for a quiet time with God don't have to go to a special place. We don't need a high priest to offer sacrifices or burn incense. We can build our nest near God and enjoy daily moments in it with Him. It is said that Susannah Wesley, a mother of nineteen children, would simply put her apron over her head when she needed a quiet moment with God, and her children knew they should not interrupt her.

Does your soul yearn for the courts of the Lord? Do you feel the daily need for your quiet time alone with Him? I have a plaque in my kitchen that says, "Time is a daily treasure, which attracts many robbers." Don't let anything rob you of your daily time with God.

❖ Find a regular time and place to build a "nest" just for you and God.

Help me, Father, to discipline myself to have quality time with You each day.

21
Irresponsible Parenting

Read: Deuteronomy 6:4-8
Key verse: You shall teach them diligently to your sons.

The brown-headed cowbird is North America's only parasitic species, laying its eggs in other birds' nests. The female will lay one egg in a nest already containing eggs, and will occasionally remove one of the host eggs, eating it before she lays her own and goes on her way. The baby cowbird is bigger and stronger than the other babies, so it usually gets the greater share of the food and may crowd the other young out of the nest. Cowbirds don't build nests – they just find a nest with its owner gone for a few minutes. Females lay an average of forty eggs a year. They have no responsibility in raising their young; they let other birds do it.

Do you know any parents who neglect raising their children? Even if people supply their children with the basic necessities of life, or perhaps provide costly luxuries, many mothers and fathers depend on the church or school to teach their children the most important values of life. Establishing a home and raising children is hard work. As a kindergarten teacher, I could tell which children were being taught manners, morals, and Christian values. Some parents were hoping grandparents would teach those things – the parents didn't want to assume that responsibility.

Baby cowbirds grow up to do exactly as their parents did. Children usually do the same thing, and that can be a tragic cycle.

It takes a firm commitment from dedicated parents to be responsible and raise their children in a Christian home.

❖ Teach your children Bible verses, pray with them, go to church with them, and sing "Jesus Loves Me" with them.

> *Father, don't let me ever be lackadaisical in teaching my children about You.*

(COWBIRDS)

22
Feathers Are Letters

Read: Psalm 119:89-106

Key verse: Your word is a lamp to my feet and a light to my path.

My kindergarten students were always bringing in feathers they found at home or on the playground. They learned that feathers are unique to birds. (Only birds have feathers – bats can fly, but have no feathers.) The children also learned that feathers not only enable birds to fly, but they help us identify birds and they keep the birds warm in winter and cool in summer.

My students also enjoyed a little poem titled "If You Find a Little Feather":

> If you find a little feather,
> a little white feather,
> a soft and tickly feather,
>   it's for you.
>
> A feather is a letter
> from a bird.

The poem goes on to say the bird wants you to think of him and never forget him.

God's Word is a letter to us. He tells us what He has done for us in the past and all He wants to do for us now and in the future. He reminds us that His Word stands firm in heaven, and that His laws are perfect. He instructs us in practical living, and He tells us clearly how He sent Jesus to die so we can spend eternity with Him. God's letter asks us lovingly to think of Him and never forget Him.

Five-year-olds are thrilled to find feathers. Are we just as excited about reading God's letter to us each day?

❖ Read the Bible through this year or invite your neighbors to a Bible study.

Thank You, Lord, for Your Word and for the ability and freedom to read it.

23
Unique Birds

Read: Ecclesiastes 3:4
Key verse: A time to weep and a time to laugh.

Didja hear the one about the two birds sitting at the side of a large puddle of oil? They see a worm on the other side. One bird flies over; the other one swims through the puddle. Which one gets to the worm first? The one that swims, of course, because "de oily boid gets de woim."

Your kindergartner might like this one: What happens to a duck when he flies upside down? He quacks up.

The reason hummingbirds hum is apparently because they forgot the words.

And the way to catch a unique bird? Unique up on it!

My favorite bird joke is about the two preachers who bought parrots. One preacher got a male parrot which only would say in a raucous squawk, "Let's neck." The other preacher got a female parrot which said in a pious little squeak, "Let's pray." They put the birds in the same cage, hoping the male would imitate the female. He immediately squawked, "Let's neck." She responded meekly, "My prayers are answered."

I hope you are chuckling. Proverbs 17:22 says, "A joyful heart is good medicine." Of all people, we Christians have reasons to be joyful. Yes, life is going to have sorrow, but our Savior has overcome death and the grave, and our God can bring good from any circumstance. The Bible tells us to rejoice in the Lord always (Phil. 4:4). A sour Christian who complains a lot is not a winsome witness. So learn a few good jokes and brighten the corner where you are!

❖ Develop a plan for monitoring your complaining; are you fun to be around?

Convict me, Holy Spirit, when I start to grumble. Let me be a cheerful Christian.

24
Under His Wings

Read: Psalm 91
Key verse: And under His wings you may seek refuge.

As a child, I watched with fascination as a mother hen, sensing danger in the barnyard, would signal her chicks to come to her. She would settle down over them until the danger passed, and then little heads would begin to peep out through her feathers. Soon the babies were scurrying all around her, but staying nearby just in case. I often wondered what might happen if the hen weren't alert to the dangers of hawks or foxes. What if the babies didn't recognize her alarm signal, or what if they chose to ignore her? What would happen when they grew too big to get under her wings?

Baby chicks quickly outgrow their need to run to mama for protection, but we never get so old or self-sufficient that we no longer need God. According to this Psalm, He is our protector, our refuge, our deliverer, our rescuer, and our satisfaction. He promises to be with us in trouble, and we can depend on His faithfulness. But what happens if we ignore Him or get so far away that we don't hear His call?

When the hawks of life swoop down on us, we need to be close to our Most High God.

❖ Write down one or two times you have run to God for refuge in the past.

Father, thank You for being my shelter. Make me keenly aware of Your warnings.

25
Significant Sparrows

Read: Matthew 10:21-31
Key verse: You are more valuable than many sparrows.

Sparrows were of little significance in Jesus' day, and there were probably many of them. The common house sparrow is considered a nuisance here in the United States. It is not a native bird – it perhaps could be considered an illegal alien. It is not pretty, does not have a real song, builds messy nests in public places, and destroys the nests of small songbirds. Sparrows are frequently chased away from bird feeders by people who want to attract more desirable birds.

And yet, Jesus said not one sparrow falls to the earth apart from the Father's will. If even a sparrow has significance to God, how much more do we matter to Him? He actually knows the number of hairs on our heads! The details of our lives are important to Him. What matters to us matters to Him, and He wants us to talk to Him about it.

❖ Tell the people around you why they are significant to you and to God.

Father, I am in awe that among the billions of people on earth, You see me, You know me, and You love me.

26
Mockingbird Music

Read: 1 Corinthians 12:4-31
Key verse: Now there are varieties of gifts but the same spirit.

Although mockingbirds are gifted singers with a beautiful song of their own, they are best known for their ability to mimic. Not only do they copy other birds, but they even can mimic a dog's barking, a squeaky wheel, and many other sounds in their environment. The mockingbird sings loudly and frequently sings all night. Mockingbirds generally have a hundred or more different song types in their repertoires, and they add new sounds as they hear them. The males usually repeat a song type three or more times in rapid succession before switching to a new song.

God has made each of us unique, with special abilities and talents we can use to His glory. When we rush around trying to do everything we see others doing, or we refuse to use our own gifts because we think others can do things better, we miss the opportunity God gave us to give glory to Him in our own special way.

We can't all be wrens or larks, but if we offer our services out of love for God and others, we will make a joyful noise – not just a loud one.

❖ Use your unique talent to bring God glory today. Or, instead of listening to Christian music, sing your own praises to Him.

Father, thank You for making me special. Give me eyes to see the talents of others, and help me encourage them to use those abilities.

27
Robin Redbreast

Read: Colossians 1:13-23
Key verse: Having made peace through the blood of His cross.

When I was a child, Daddy often sang for me an old song about how the robin got its red breast. The lyrics described how a bird flew around the head of Jesus as He was bleeding on the cross. The bird was attempting to fan Christ's thorn-pierced brow to relieve His pain. But the bird's chest got blood on it, and to this day, according to the song, the robin has a red breast. The Bible does not confirm this story, so we consider it a sweet little legend.

The Bible does describe, however, Christ's bleeding and suffering on the cross, and we believe it as truth. There is a danger today, even as in Paul's day, of adding things to the bible's teaching. Most modern cults have some elements of biblical truth, but we must ask God for wisdom and discernment. Paul's letter to the Colossians was intended to combat heresy and to spell out clearly what Christians believe. Only through the blood of Christ do we have redemption.

❖ Whenever you see a robin, thank Jesus for being willing to shed His blood.

> *Father God, thank You for Your infallible, inerrant Word, which contains only truth.*

28
Flocking Together

Read: John 17:13-20

Key verse: They are not of the world, even as I am not of the world.

Did your mother ever say, "Birds of a feather flock together" when she wanted you to examine the type of people with whom you were spending time? Most of us probably learned even in elementary school that we tended to behave like our friends. Peer pressure still dictates how our children dress, talk, and spend their time.

Bird watchers have observed that even on bird refuges where hundreds of thousands of ducks and geese gather, each species stays pretty much with its own kind. Flocking aids birds in three basic activities: feeding, travel, and defense. Large numbers of birds gathering around an abundant food source serve as a conspicuous signal to other birds searching for food. Some birds, such as American white pelicans, engage in cooperative fish drives. Traveling flocks are almost always exclusively one species. It's interesting that Arctic shore birds flock in different age groups when migrating. Some birds form defensive groups quickly in response to a common threat, and may include more than one species. Aggressive flocks discourage raptors or nest robbers.

As Christians, we are to be *in* the world as light and salt, and yet not *of* the world. We cannot stay inside our churches, enjoying the fellowship with other believers, and ignore those out in the community who don't know Christ. But we do need to be careful that we don't succumb to the world's temptations – that we don't start acting like unbelievers.

❖ Ask yourself if your conversation and behavior change, depending on with whom you're "flocking."

> *Oh God, I thank You for my Christian friends, but make me aware of those around me who don't know You.*

29
Who Tells the Wild Geese?

Read: Song of Solomon 2:11-13
Key verse: For behold, the winter is past.

When winter days grow long and dreary and we tire of cold and snow, we can be encouraged by Solomon's reminder of how glorious spring is – the time of flowers and singing of birds. I do appreciate my sturdy feathered friends who brighten the gray days of winter – cardinals, chickadees, and blue jays – but I'm always excited to welcome back the bluebirds, the hummingbirds, and the other migratory birds. Then I realize again how awesome our God is – He can direct robins from my yard to Florida and back to my yard again – even back to the same tree where they hatched the previous summer!

In the fall, robins gather in groups as though they are talking things over – "Is it time to go? Are we ready?" I like to think they are waiting for a word from God. One of my favorite poems is "Something Told the Wild Geese" by Rachel Field.

> Something told the wild geese, it was time to go.
> Though the fields lay golden, something whispered, – "Snow."
> Leaves were green and stirring, berries luster-glossed,
> But beneath warm feathers something cautioned, – "Frost."
> All the sagging orchards, steamed with amber spice,
> But each wild breast stiffened, at remembered ice.
> Something told the wild geese, it was time to fly, –
> Summer sun was on their wings, winter in their cry.

I'd rather think some One told the wild geese that it was time. God controls the seasons perfectly. Even birds obey Him.

❖ Take time today to smell a flower and listen to a bird sing.

Almighty God, how great is Your faithfulness. You always produce a spring after a winter!

30
Stealing Magpies

Read: Titus 2:6-12

Key verse: Not to steal by taking things of small value. (AMP)

The Italian composer Rossini is perhaps best known for his "William Tell Overture," but he also wrote a brilliant opera, inspired by a true story, about a thieving magpie. Magpies are attracted to shiny objects and will take whatever they can find (and carry) to their bulky nests. Rossini's story involves a maid about to be executed for stealing one of her employer's silver spoons, when the spoon is found in a magpie's nest. The opera ends happily, but unfortunately in the real-life event, the magpie's nest with the spoon wasn't discovered in time.

Many people get away with stealing. In fact, some people wouldn't even consider their actions stealing, when all they do is take a few items home from the office or keep the extra change they are given accidentally. Most of us purposely would not break one of the Ten Commandments, but we interpret stealing to mean only big things – or important things. God warns us to reject all ungodliness and to live discreet, honest lives. My mother used to tell me that even snooping is a form of stealing, because you're invading someone's privacy. Perhaps the best rule of thumb is: would I do this if Jesus were standing beside me? Could I rationalize my deed to Him?

❖ Treat yourself to a recording of "The Thieving Magpie," then thank God for music and the composers who write it.

Holy Spirit, tweak my conscience when I'm tempted to steal "small things."

31
Familiar Voices

Read: John 10:1-5
Key verse: The sheep follow Him because they know His voice.

Some of the most fascinating bird research in the world takes place at the Cornell Lab of Ornithology in Ithaca, New York (For a full description of the lab's programs, go to their excellent Web site at http://birds.cornell.edu.) In one of their more famous experiments, scientists raised baby bluebirds by hand in a sound-isolation chamber. The young birds showed little interest when songs of various birds were piped in. But when the bluebird song was played, they reacted strongly to these unfamiliar notes and quickly learned to sing them.

Jesus tells the Pharisees in a parable that He is a good shepherd and that His sheep listen for His voice, they recognize His voice, and they follow Him. In a world where many voices clamor for our attention, it is essential that we listen *for* our Lord's voice, we listen *to* what He says, and then we obey Him.

Something deep within the young bluebirds responded to the voice of their own kind. Something deep in our hearts longs to respond to the call of our Creator. We may not understand all about theology or doctrine, but we can simply say yes when we hear Jesus' voice. Then as we follow Him, He will teach us to sing a new song.

❖ Make sure that in your quiet time with God each day, you take a few minutes just to listen.

Lord Jesus, I hear Your voice, and I respond. Teach me what I need to know.

32
Wings of Faith

Read: Hebrews 11:1-3
Key verse: Now faith is the assurance of things hoped for, the conviction of things not seen.

One of my favorite pieces of poetry is this one by Victor Hugo:

> Be like the bird, who
> Halting in his flight
> On limb too slight,
> Feels it give way beneath him,
> Yet sings – knowing he has wings.

Our faith gives us "wings" – the sure confidence that when our world begins to give way beneath us, God will be there for us. Our hopes may be shattered, but our souls are safe. When we have Christ, we have everything we need. We should not worry that another limb will be too slight or that another crisis will come – we just ride out the storm with the One who holds us up.

I have a picture that shows a chickadee sitting in a man's hand to eat seeds. The inscription reads, "Faith is not belief without proof, but trust without reservation." May we have faith that trusts God's outstretched hands – without reservation.

❖ Exercise your wings of faith and decide to trust God's promises. Choose one to claim for today and write it down.

Oh, Father, forgive me when I forget that You have told me not to worry, that the everlasting arms of God are beneath me.

33
Future Bird Lovers

Read: Psalm 78:2-8
Key verse: That they should teach them to their children.

I recently read an article about adult mentors who study birds with young people. One teen commented that he felt blessed to spend time with adults who stimulated his love for birds. He considered these mentors to be some of the most important people in his life. The article pointed out that even though young people today have access to a wealth of information in libraries, Web sites, and educational programs, the key ingredient is an adult who willingly shares his or her enthusiasm and knowledge about birds.

I began to wonder if we adult Christians ever think of ourselves as mentors to young people – sharing our enthusiasm for the Lord and our knowledge about living the Christian life. Do we assume they aren't interested if they don't ask us questions? Do we make simple statements to pique their curiosity? For example, as a bird lover, I can point out to my grandchildren how God gives birds ways to protect themselves, or how He helps them migrate. We all can relate to young people around us in our own unique ways. As we share our time and hobbies, we can emphasize our love of God and the importance of His place in our lives. We may not feel led to teach a children's Sunday school class; leading a children's choir may not be our talent. But whatever we do can be a meaningful spiritual lesson for the young people around us.

❖ Offer to help with your church's youth program, or share a talent with the kids in your neighborhood.

Father, I want to encourage a child's love for You. Show me the best way to do it.

34
Thrilling Moments

Read: John 15:9-17

Key verse: These things I have spoken to you so that My joy may be in you.

My favorite backyard bird is the Carolina wren. One spring day I was planting flowers under a large forsythia bush when a male wren flew into the branches near my head and began to sing.

I sat quietly and watched his little body throb with the joy of his song. He flew away a few minutes later, and I hurried into my kitchen to tell my daughters about the special moment. "Girls," I called, "the most wonderful thing just happened!" And as I described the incident, they began to roll their eyes as only teenage girls do, and said, "It doesn't take much to thrill you, Mother, does it?"

Maybe not, but God loves me so much that He knows what little gifts will thrill me – things *you* might not even notice. Few things thrill me more than watching Canada geese settle down on a meadow, or hearing a meadowlark sing on a spring morning. God tailor-makes my blessings, and everyday He plans little love gifts from His heart to mine. He knows and loves *you* just as intimately, and delights in thrilling you, too. Are you watching for God's personal gifts to you each day? Do you say, "Oh, Father, I love You, too" when you see them?

❖ Watch for a handpicked gift from God today. Write down what He gives you.

   Father, thank You for knowing what gifts thrill me, and thank You for giving them to me.

(CAROLINA WREN)

35
Wise Old Owl

Read: James 1:19-26

Key verse: Everyone must be quick to hear, slow to speak, and slow to anger.

Most of us have heard this rhyme:

> A wise old owl sat in an oak.
> The more he saw, the less he spoke.
> The less he spoke, the more he heard.
> Why can't we be like that wise old bird?

In today's scripture reading, James tells us to be quick to listen but slow to speak. Why do women seem to have a harder time with this than men? I taught kindergarten for many years, and even at that age, it was obvious that little girls like to chatter not only *with* each other but *about* each other as well.

Jesus taught in Matthew 12:36-37 that we will give an account for every careless word we have spoken. Just what *is* a careless word? Could it be words that show I care less about another person's reputation than I do my own? Perhaps it means wasting time chattering when I could be saying something meaningful about my relationship to God. Maybe I could use those words to say a prayer with someone who is hurting. Words are powerful, and we need to use them carefully.

❖ Watch for opportunities to say helpful words today.

Lord, help me know when to speak up and when to be quiet.

36
Geese Appreciation

Read: 1 Thessalonians 5:11-23
Key verse: Encourage one another and build up one another.

Few people can resist watching in awe when a large "V" of Canada geese soars overhead. The sights – and the sound – are inspiring. Scientists tell us the honking is meant to encourage each other, especially the goose out in front who is working the hardest. We also know the geese take turns leading the formation while others get rest farther back in the line.

Geese are loyal to each other. If a goose gets sick or injured, at least one other goose stays with it until it is strong enough to fly again.

What lessons can a church learn from geese? Certainly, we should be encouraging our leaders, especially our pastors. Moreover, we should be willing to do our part, even assuming leadership if the Lord leads us. We should take care of each other – helping, giving, and praying.

One final lesson from Canada geese – they mate for life. Wouldn't it be a powerful testimony if church folks always did the same?

❖ Call or write a church leader – tell him or her you appreciate him or her.

> *Father, thank You for all those who work in Your kingdom. Show me how I can do my part.*

37
Greedy Woodpeckers

Read: Acts 5:1-11
Key verse: You have not lied to men but to God.

A folktale tells the story of a hungry old man walking through the woods, when he came to the cottage of a widow and asked her for food. She baked a cake for him, but the cake turned out so well she wanted it for herself. She told the man to wait while she baked him a smaller cake. When that cake turned out to be even bigger, she told the man to leave – she wasn't willing to share either cake. The man stomped his foot, and the woman's red cap, black dress, and white apron became feathers, and she flew off into the woods crying, "Cheat, cheat."

The cry of the redheaded woodpecker always reminds me of how greed can ruin lives. Ananias and Sapphira in today's reading died immediately when confronted with their sin – lying to God about their money. Today's newspapers tell of corporate greed and the slide into ruin by those who succumb to the lust for wealth. Paul warned us that the love of money is the root of all kinds of evil (1 Tim. 6:10), and Jesus said that a man's life doesn't consist in the abundance of his possessions (Luke 12:15). In fact, Jesus had more to say about money than almost any other topic. God knows how easily we are tripped up by money and the lust for things money can buy.

❖ Share your riches in Christ Jesus. Give an anonymous gift to a needy person.

Lord, forgive me for hugging my blessings so tightly that I can't see the needs of others.

(REDHEADED WOODPECKER)

38
Unanswered Questions

Read: Isaiah 55:8-11

Key verse: So are My ways higher than your ways.

While reading books about birds, I frequently see the words *we don't know.* (I'm sure the same thing is true about other animal research.) Even with the newest technology and scientific investigations, there are still many questions we human beings want answered.

For example, why do birds take dust baths? It has been suggested that dusting removes excess moisture and oil from feathers or that it flushes out parasites, but we don't know for sure.

The way birds interact with each other has many mysteries. When house sparrows fight, why do males only attack males, and females only attack females? Does the simple sparrow have some code of honor?

Another unanswered question: are birds actually communicating with each other when they chirp and sing? We don't know. And, of course, we probably will never know all the wonders of migration.

We human beings also have many questions about our own lives. Why does God let children suffer and die? Is it fair that Christians can be poor when wicked people prosper? How can God bring good from tragedies? There are many answers we will never know, but we can, in simple faith, let God be God. He is sovereign – He knows everything, and when we're with Him for eternity, the answers will no longer concern us.

❖ Take your questions to God. Be honest with your feelings.

> *Creator of the Universe, I thank You for being big enough to handle my doubts and questions. Let me rest in Your infinite wisdom.*

39
Extinction Dangers

Read: Isaiah 40:6-8
Key verse: The word of our God stands forever.

In the last two hundred years or so, some seventy to eighty species of birds have become extinct. Probably most of them have disappeared because of man's activities. The dodo and great auk were hunted by man; the passenger pigeon may have died out because of the loss of its habitat. Even though the federal government got involved at the beginning of the twentieth century, and while we are being more careful with pollution of the environment and destruction of natural habitats, there are many other species in danger of extinction. In 2002, there were seventy-eight birds just from North America on the endangered list. Even the bald eagle has been on that list for a period of time. There are programs to protect and build up populations of endangered birds, such as whooping cranes and the Californian condor.

In today's reading, God assures us that His Word will stand forever – it can never become extinct. Even in those countries where Bibles are forbidden, people are risking their lives to read and treasure the Good News. The Bible continues to be the world's best-selling book, but even if it disappeared from every library and home, its words are hidden in the hearts of Christians; we still could put one together again. We never will see another dodo, but we always will have God's Word.

❖ Memorize a Bible verse today.

Thank You, Lord, for Your Word. Help me to treasure it and keep it alive in my heart.

40
Times of Turbulence

Read: Hebrews 6:13-19
Key verse: This hope we have as an anchor.

The grebe, a water bird resembling a duck, builds a unique nest designed to escape land predators as well as turbulent floods. The grebe begins the nest by bringing up mud and plants from the bottom of a lake. These are then piled on a little platform of green floating stalks. The platform, just large enough to hold the eggs and the mother grebe, appears as a mass of dead vegetation. But the grebe attaches this floating nest around the stalks of nearby cattails or reeds. This step both anchors it and allows it to bob up and down with the waves.

As Christians who live in an uncertain world with dangers lurking nearby and evils threatening to flood our existence, we need to remember that we are anchored on the sure Rock that is Jesus Christ. He alone can hold us steady in uncertain times. A plunging stock market, threats of terrorism, devastating hurricanes – all these things can cause us to bob up and down, but our anchor will hold. God uses the traumas in our personal lives – illness, joblessness, family concerns – to teach us that He's in control and that He will keep us from being swept away.

❖ Write down what you have already experienced with the Lord as your anchor.

> *Lord Jesus, You are my rock, my anchor, and my eternal hope. I praise Your name.*

(GREBE)

41
Quenching Thirsts

Read: John 4:1-15
Key verse: But whoever takes a drink of the water that I will give them shall never, no never be thirsty anymore. (AMP)

Most birds need to drink frequently. Small birds may sip drops of dew or rain off the vegetation. Others such as swallows collect water as they skim across the surface of lakes. Most birds dip their beaks into water, then tip their heads back. Pigeons can drink by sucking up water with a pumping action.

Jesus told the Samaritan woman at the well that He could give her water that would quench her thirst, and she would never be thirsty again. She was so amazed at His teaching that she left her water jar and went to get her friends and neighbors.

Some of the ways we can drink of the living water Jesus offers are by giving Him our lives, reading His word, praying and communing with Him, worshiping with other Christians, and being obedient to His leading. We can have our own spring of water welling and bubbling up within us when we have a personal encounter with Jesus. Our lives can be so full that we want to share the source of this living water with our friends and neighbors.

❖ Tell Jesus today that you want the water only He can give.

Father, thank You for quenching my spiritual thirst. Help me to be obedient in telling others.

42
Meaningful Names

Read: Philippians 2:5-11
Key verse: For this reason also, God highly exalted Him and bestowed on Him the name which is above every name.

The names of many birds give a clue to their appearance or behavior. It's obvious how the red-winged blackbird or yellow-bellied sapsucker got their names. Snow geese and snowy egrets are white, as you might expect. A ruddy turnstone is a water bird with reddish legs, and it turns over stones or shells on the beach looking for food. The limpkin walks with a slow, crippled appearance. Cattle egrets are most frequently seen in pastures near cattle. The chickadee says its name, while the catbird's mewing call is easy to identify.

The names of Jesus tell us about His character and His interactions with man. My Bible lists over two hundred names/descriptions of Jesus Christ, from both the Old and New Testaments. Just reading through His names give a clear picture of who He is and what He does.

Over seven hundred years before the birth of Christ, Isaiah said, "She shall call His name 'Immanuel'" (which means "God with us"). When Jesus walked on this earth, He was called Teacher, Master, Son of David, and King. He described Himself as the Good Shepherd, the True Vine, the Way, the Truth, and the Life. On a personal level, He is my Refuge, my Rock, and my Hope. But when I am most aware of my sins, my favorite names for Him are Savior, Redeemer, and Friend.

❖ Make a list of ten names of Jesus that are meaningful to you.

How I thank You, Lord, that Jesus is the sweetest name I know, and He's just the same as His lovely name.

43
Hiding from God

Read: Genesis 3:1-13
Key verse: So I hid myself.

In the classic children's book, *The Story About Ping,* a young duck living on a houseboat in China learns some valuable lessons. Knowing he will be spanked if he's the last to board the houseboat one evening, he chooses to hide. He is captured by a family who plans to have a duck dinner. Only the soft heart of a child saves him, and he is never again slow to respond to his master's call.

Kindergarteners understand the lesson to come when called, and they shudder at the nearly disastrous result of Ping's hiding from his family. But how many adults try to tune out God's calling them to repentance or to a deeper walk with Him? How many Christians choose to run from God and ignore His protection when they want their own way? Adam tried to hide from God after choosing to sin; it didn't work. David explains in Psalm 139 that we can't hide anything – even our thoughts – from God.

The wonderful truth is that even when we sin and wish we *could* hide, God comes looking for us – not to punish us, but to forgive us and restore our relationship with Him. We make the choice whether or not to accept it. Ping nearly lost his life; the stakes are even higher for us.

❖ Ask yourself in what ways you are trying to hide from God.

Forgive my foolishness, Lord. Make me want to run to You, not away from You.

44
Useful Recipes

Read: 2 Peter 1:2-11
Key verse: Learn to know Him better and better.

Here are two recipes all birders should know: (1) To attract hummingbirds to your yard, plant trumpet vines or red petunias. To keep them coming, fill a commercial hummingbird feeder with fresh sugar water (four parts water to one part sugar). (2) For birds who like suet in the winter, use this easy recipe: mix one cup peanut butter, one cup shortening, one cup flour, and four cups cornmeal. Pack into a commercial suet holder or use a mesh bag. Hang outdoors near bird feeders.

Recipes can be very useful when you want to produce something specific. There are even recipes in the Bible for producing mature Christians. The main ingredients are Bible study, prayer, and fellowship with other Christians. Just as physical fitness demands daily exercise, spiritual maturity requires consistent training as well. Someone has said that growing strong in our faith demands disciplined devotion, definite direction, and diligent determination. The more we learn about Christ, the more we want to obey Him. Paul told Timothy (1 Tim. 4:8) that exercising spiritually helps us not only in this life but in the next one, too. When Christ returns to take us into His eternal kingdom, He will finish the work He started in us, and only *His* recipe will make us finally perfect.

❖ Make sure your recipe for Christian growth includes adequate time with God's Word.

> *Father, help me to take time to be holy. As the old hymn says, I want to speak oft with my Lord and make friends of God's children.*

45
Getting One's Attention

Read: Jeremiah 31:1-3
Key verse: I have drawn you with lovingkindness.

Male birds will go to great length to attract females. Cranes are noted for their wild courtship dances, while many birds of prey have remarkable aerial displays. Some birds display outstanding plumages; the peacock's fanning of its magnificent tail feathers is perhaps the most spectacular. Some birds make loud, unusual calls or show off their skills, such as hanging upside down from a branch. The chickadee tries to impress a prospective mate with singing, cardinals feed each other, and some birds offer nesting material during courtship. The most bizarre display is probably the great frigatebird's red pouch, which can be puffed out to the size of a football beneath the bird's chin.

God wants us to notice *Him*, and He has many ways of getting our attention. Sometimes He woos us gently by giving us little love gifts or by whispering comforting thoughts when we need them. Other times He speaks through sorrow or despair. He displays Himself in the power and beauty of nature; He shows us His wisdom in the perfect laws of science.

God loves us, and He wants us to know it. He is patient and will do whatever He can to draw us to Him. But He will not force us to choose Him – He wants us to come willingly.

❖ Ask yourself what God has been doing to get your attention. Have you responded to Him?

> *I know, Lord, that You are the Lover of my soul; thank You for drawing me to You.*

(GREAT FRIGATEBIRD)

46
Hospitals

Read: Isaiah 37:1-4
Key verse: He tore his clothes, covered himself with sackcloth, and went into the house of the Lord.

My daughter found a baby robin too young to live on its own, so she took it to a nearby wild bird clinic. The workers there assured her that this insignificant, helpless creature would be hand fed, kept clean and comfortable, and released only when able to live in its natural surroundings. There were other birds that were sick, injured, or recovering from being covered with oil. All of them were receiving professional care, along with necessary medicines and X-rays. There was no charge for the care given the little robin, and in fact, the clinic later sent my daughter a postcard telling her when and where the bird was released.

The church should be just such a haven for hurting, wounded people – a spiritual hospital for all kinds of needs. All of us are sinners who need cleansing, and many of us have been crippled by circumstances – some beyond our control and others of our own choosing. In today's reading, King Hezekiah needed a place of refuge during a difficult time, and so he went into the house of the Lord. The outside world didn't change, but Hezekiah had his spiritual and emotional needs met before he went out to face his life.

❖ Offer your time as a volunteer to help hurting people in your church, local nursing home, or prison.

Thank You, Lord, for my church. Help it always to be a safe sanctuary for people who are hurting.

47
Crow Wisdom

Read: Proverbs 3
Key verse: How blessed is the man who finds wisdom.

We usually think of owls as the "wise" bird, but it is actually the crow that appears to be the genius of the bird family. Scientists have determined that crows have the largest brains relative to body size of any bird. These birds are intelligent enough to make and use tools; a biologist reported how crows used twigs to extract insects from trees and then saved the twigs to be used again. Another writer described crows stealing bait and fish from ice fishermen. The birds grasped untended line and pulled, stepping on the slack to keep it from slipping back into the water, repeating this trick until lunch popped from the hole. And in a very old story, Aesop described how a crow devised a way to get a drink by putting pebbles in an urn until the small amount of water finally rose to the top.

The wisest man who ever lived said the fear of God is the beginning of wisdom. Solomon went on to say the man who knows right from wrong and has common sense is happier than the man who is immensely rich (TLB). When you search for wisdom in God's Word, then work at applying it, and consistently discipline yourself to live as God asks, you discover that no worldly success can compare with the joy of the Christian life.

It doesn't take great intelligence to believe in Jesus; it takes simple faith. Those who accept Christ's offer of everlasting life are actually the wisest of all. Wise men still seek Him, and not just at Christmas.

❖ Read the first nine chapters of Proverbs. Underline the benefits of wisdom as you read.

I need Your wisdom today, Lord. Thank You for making it available.

48
Endurance of Chimney Swifts

Read: Hebrews 6:10-15
Key verse: And so, having patiently waited, he obtained the promise.

Chimney swifts display amazing endurance. They are airborne almost constantly – eating, courting, bathing, and gathering nesting materials – all done while flying hundreds of miles a day. There's actually a reason why they seldom stop until going into chimneys an hour or so before sunset. The reason is that they belong to a scientific category of birds known as "Apodidae" which means "without feet." Swifts do have feet, but they're so small and weak that if a swift lands on the ground, he has a difficult time getting airborne again.

Chimney swifts know instinctively that they need to keep moving. We human beings, however, have to work at endurance. The writer of Hebrews 10:36 says we need patience and endurance so we may perform and fully accomplish the will of God, and he gives us in Hebrews 11 a list of people who demonstrated endurance. He urges *us* to run with endurance the race that is set before us (Heb. 12:1).

Satan deliberately slows us down and tries to ground us completely. We can get side-tracked with family situations. I know of a talented Christian who dropped out of all church work for a full year so she could plan her daughter's wedding. Or we let illness keep us idle; even when we've recovered, we don't get back into the Lord's work. And children can become great excuses – we're too busy with all their activities to do anything for the Lord.

With determination and prayer, we can become airborne again. There are saints all around us who already have proven it can be done.

❖ List ten people whose Christian endurance you admire.

Father, keep me moving with steadfast endurance toward the goals You have set for me.

(CHIMNEY SWIFT)

49
Looking for Signs

Read: John 2:1-11
Key verse: This beginning of His signs, Jesus did in Cana of Galilee...and His disciples believed in Him.

Many times in literature as well as history, birds have been used as signs or omens. Perhaps the best known bird in the Bible is the dove, which Noah sent out to look for a sign that the floodwaters had receded. There was great rejoicing when the dove came back with an olive leaf.

In 1492 Columbus's men were planning mutiny in their fear and frustration over not finding land. But a man-o-war bird flew over their ships, and the weary sailors correctly surmised that they must be nearing land.

Farmers know when Canada geese head north that winter weather is only about six weeks away – a sign to get the crops in.

Jesus performed many signs and miracles to prove He was God's son – the first sign coming at a wedding when He turned water into wine. His disciples believed in Him then, and after other signs, many more people believed.

What sign led *you* to believe in Jesus? The disciple Thomas needed to see the nail prints in Jesus' hands. Are you still waiting for a sign? Just look around at the changed lives of those who believe in Him!

❖ Read John 20:24-31.

Almighty God, thank You for all the signs that Jesus is who He said He is, and thank You that He is coming again.

50
Judgmental Cardinals

Read: Romans 2:1-6
Key verse: You have no excuse, everyone of you who passes judgment.

A female cardinal slammed into my sliding glass door last week. She sat on the deck several minutes, obviously stunned and in pain. I was amazed to see a group of cardinals – both male and female – move from the nearby feeders and settle down on the deck around the injured bird. I was touched by their apparent concern and sympathy, until two of them suddenly attacked the helpless bird, pecking at her and bumping her. They appeared to be angry with her for just sitting there. Then the group flew back to the feeders, leaving the injured bird alone.

I thought of Job, whose friends came to him in his misery and instead of comforting him, they tormented him with their words and attitudes. Then I wondered about how we Christians treat fellow believers who are wounded in body or spirit. We might take a casserole to the person who broke a bone, we might send a note to a depressed friend, but how do we respond to the one whose recent sin or lack of faith has crippled him or her? Do we "peck" at them by pointing fingers or gossiping? Or do we demonstrate God's love and forgiveness, coming along side them to mentor, lift up, and comfort them?

❖ Examine your attitudes – are you guilty of being judgmental?

> *Father, make me genuinely concerned for Christians who are hurting, and show me what I can do to encourage them.*

51
Where Are You, Birdie?

Read: 1 Peter 2:9-12

Key verse: Keep your behavior excellent...so that...they may glorify God.

Serious birdwatchers know that a clue to a bird's identity is where the bird prefers to eat, drink, and spend its time. Robins are one of the best known birds in North America because they are usually seen on lawns and open area, whereas their cousins – towhees (or ground robins) – prefer dense thickets where they scratch through dead leaves; you usually hear them before you see them. Orioles prefer the treetops, and tree sparrows are seen in fields or lawns. Cardinals like their food on the ground; chickadees go happily to feeders. Some birds will drink from a bird bath or puddle; others are happier with streams.

A clue to identifying Christians can also be where they prefer to spend their time. It is possible, of course, to be a Christian without going to church or Bible studies, but most Christians are more comfortable in these places than in bars or casinos. Christians can also be found in hospitals, nursing homes, and prisons – ministering to people who are hurting. Many Christians are like those shy birds that stay in the woods – quietly doing what God has given them to do without calling any attention to themselves. Some serve as prayer warriors in their homes.

Are we where God wants us to be? Does our environment help us live like Christians?

❖ List the places you could be found in a week's time. Do those places honor God?

Holy God, convict me when I'm not where I should be, and vice versa.

52
Remarkable Feathers

Read: Psalm 18:1-3
Key verse: The Lord is my rock.

God's attention to detail has always fascinated me, and a bird's feathers are a good example of a Master Designer. A feather is a marvel of aeronautical engineering. Besides allowing birds the greatest flight techniques among flying animals, feathers also form an insulating layer around the body, keeping the body waterproofed and providing color for camouflage as well as recognition. Feathers make it possible for birds to ride effortlessly for hours on the wind, to travel speeds more than one hundred miles per hour, to hover and fly backward, and even to "fly" underwater. The outer feathers can be very strong with interlocking barbs, while the down feathers underneath, although soft, offer the most efficient protection against cold ever developed. Man has not been able to invent a better material for insulation.

Only our awesome God could have created the feathers for the world's variety of birds. Each bird has exactly the kind, shape, size, and color of feathers it needs.

Can you trust God for the details of your life? Don't you think He knows what you need even before you do? The world cannot invent any better solutions to your deepest concerns. God alone is able to do more than our minds can conceive.

❖ Find the old hymn "Only Trust Him" and sing it aloud.

> *Almighty God, I praise You for knowing all the details of my life, and I thank You for loving me so much that You care about those details.*

53
Seeking and Finding

Read: Matthew 7:7-14
Key verse: Keep on seeking, and you will find. (AMP)

In the spring of 1851, a new species of warbler was captured on the Ohio farm of naturalist Jared P. Kirtland. For over half a century ornithologists tried to solve the mystery of the origin of the Kirtland's warbler. The bird was known to winter in the Bahama Islands, but the question was, where was its summer home and breeding territory?

In the summer of 1903, a student found a dead bird in the pine barrens of northern Michigan and took it to his professor, who immediately set off by train, boat, and foot to see if he could find another one. On the first day of his search, he not only heard the beautiful Kirtland's warbler, but he found its nest. It was like finding the last lost piece of a large jigsaw puzzle. The jack pine forests of Michigan are the species' exclusive habitat. Looking for this rare bird anywhere else is a waste of time.

Jesus told His followers that those who keep on seeking will find the straight and narrow way that leads to eternal life. Although the wide and spacious path is much more attractive and easier to find, many people are willing to humble themselves and accept God's simple plan of salvation when it is presented to them. Jesus said that He is the only way to God the Father (John 14:6); looking anywhere else is futile.

❖ Be ready to help a seeker find Jesus; share how you became a Christian.

Lord Jesus, thank You for taking my sin away and making me fit to stand before God.

(KIRTLAND'S WARBLER)

54
Luring an Oriole

Read: Ephesians 6:10-17

Key verse: Put on the full armor of God so that you will be able to stand firm against the schemes of the devil.

I don't have orioles in my yard, and I would really enjoy their flashy beauty as well as their song. So I have a plan. I have discovered a way I can lure them to stay nearby. I am going to put out oranges smeared with grape jelly – this will appeal to their appetites. And I know orioles use string in their pouchlike nests, so I will cut lengths of thread and yarn to dangle in nearby bushes. I will be helpful in my attempt to control where the birds stay.

Satan has been observing *my* behavior and desires. He knows just what he can use to lure me into sin. He can make some things appealing to my physical appetites, and can also plant the idea that things are sensible or "fair" – the "everyone does it" syndrome. Satan wants to control me, and if he can get a temptation into my head – make me stop to consider it for a bit – he is winning the battle.

If I can get an oriole to just stop and check out an orange, or begin to pull on a piece of string, there's a good chance that I'll have orioles in my trees this summer. The lure will have worked.

❖ Watch for Satan's lures and be careful.

Oh, God, help me stand firm against temptation.

55
Feeding Babies

Read: John 6:25-35
Key verse: Then they said to Him, Lord, always give us this bread.

The inside of a baby songbird's mouth is brightly colored in red, orange, or yellow. This makes a good target for the parent, and scientists tell us it sets off a strong response to cram food into this spot. Just what do they feed their babies? Some songbirds regurgitate food into their babies' mouths until the babies' digestive tracts can handle solid food. Most songbirds feed their nestlings live insects even if the adult birds are seed-eaters. Insects are probably richer in certain proteins necessary for growth than are seeds. Those birds that feed their babies seeds carry them in their crop (a bag in the bird's throat where seeds are broken up). Baby birds are always hungry and their parents keep very busy feeding them. What a precious reminder of our Heavenly Father who says in Psalm 81:10: "Open your mouth wide and I will fill it."

God created us with a hunger for Him – an empty spot only He can fill. Satan encourages us to try many things – even wholesome activities like sports, hobbies, and being busy with good deeds – but only the Bread of Life really satisfies. Jesus tells us that only He is the true bread, which gives life to the world.

It is a paradox that feasting on the Word of God fills and satisfies us, yet gives us a craving for even more.

❖ You need spiritual nourishment – write down a plan for getting variety in your spiritual diet.

Dear God, I open my mouth – and my heart – to be fed by You.

56
Woodpecker Joy

Read: Luke 15:4-10
Key verse: There is joy in the presence of the angels of God over one sinner who repents.

I was on the phone with a friend one morning when I spotted a pileated woodpecker in the woods near our home. I quickly called to my husband and told him to come look. We were both so animated that my friend on the telephone could hear our excitement, and she wished she could see this beautiful bird herself.

Although the pileated woodpecker is not rare, it is shy and elusive, so spotting one in our area is uncommon. We were also thrilled by the bird's size and markings. One of the largest of the woodpeckers, it stands out because of its unusually shaped head. Sometimes its loud drumming on dead trees alerts birdwatchers to its presence. We go running for the binoculars when we hear it.

Our happiness over the pileated woodpecker gives us a tiny picture of heaven's rejoicing over the person who repents, who changes his mind and abhors his past sins (AMP). There is joy among the angels when they see a person come to God, when a sinner acknowledges that only Jesus Christ can save us and make us ready for heaven. Do *we* get excited when someone we care about accepts Christ as Savior? Are we enthusiastic about sharing the Good News with others?

❖ With whom could you share Christ today? Ask God to make a way for you to share the gospel.

I praise You, Lord, not only for the wonders of nature but also for the wonder of Your love.

(PILEATED WOODPECKER)

57
Sturdy Nests

Read: Matthew 7:24-27
Key verse: Yet it (the house) did not fall, for it had been founded on the rock.

A robin builds a very sturdy nest. Using mud, straw, sticks, and grass, the mother robin constructs a nearly unbreakable home for her babies. You can see old nests, which last through the winter, still lodged firmly in a tree, or you can find one that fell on the ground, still intact. I have been given many robins' nests through the years, and they're still in good condition.

The dove, on the other hand, is content to lay a few sticks across a limb and hope for the best. Wind and rain can destroy the nest. I don't have a dove's nest in my collection – it would be nearly impossible to pick one up and keep it together.

In today's reading, the wise man and the foolish man built their homes very differently. The wise man built his to last through storms. All around us today, homes are crumbling under the winds of stress and the rains of materialism. Parents may mean well and think that their children need all the latest gadgets, but no time or energy is left over for God. Many families don't go to church – they are too tired from filling their "nests." Like the dove, these families no doubt hope that their homes are strong enough for storms. But hoping isn't enough – a foundation built on the rock of God's Word is needed.

❖ Examine your family's priorities. What is most important?

> *Oh, God, I want a strong safe home built on Your Word. Show me what I need to do.*

58
Godly Protection

Read: Psalm 121
Key verse: My help comes from the Lord.

Birds will go to great lengths to protect their young. Parents are careful not to give away the location of the nest, seldom flying straight to it. Birds will attack and drive off other birds, either alone or by enlisting the help of other birds. But when the threat comes from animals or people, birds must resort to a different tactic – feigning injury. It is fascinating to watch a parent bird drop to the ground and pretend it can't fly, dragging a wing, or flopping on the ground as it leads the predator away from the nest or the helpless baby. The parent bird will even dive-bomb an animal to get its attention, then land just near enough to tempt the animal to keep following until the baby has been forgotten.

The Bible is full of references to various ways God protects His people – closing the mouths of lions, leading people to safety, and even destroying their enemies. He provides safe hiding places and protection from persecution.

But even more important than physical protection is the spiritual protection God makes available. He assures us He will give us a way to escape from temptation – we don't have to succumb to it. Peter assures us (2 Pet. 2:9) the Lord knows how to rescue the godly out of temptation, and He has far more wisdom and resources than a bird.

❖ Make a list of the ways God has protected you recently – physically and spiritually.

> *Lord, give me the wisdom to follow You when You are trying to lead me away from danger.*

59
The Crossbill's Tool

Read: 1 Timothy 4:14-16
Key verse: Do not neglect the spiritual gift within you.

An interesting legend from the Middle East tells of a little bird that twisted its beak as it tried to pry the nails from Christ's hands. The truth is God gave the red crossbill the perfect tool for wrenching open pinecone scales to get at the seeds. Crossbills are so adept at this that they can eat an estimated three thousand seeds in a day. Interestingly enough, these birds are not hatched with their unique bills – they develop as the bird feeds on pinecone seeds.

God has given each of us a tool, a tool suited for what He wants us to do in the place He has put us. Our tool, usually in the form of a talent, is to be used to glorify God, to build up and minister to the body of believers in the church, to witness to unbelievers, and to fulfill the calling God has given us. And like the crossbill's beak, our talent develops and becomes more effective the more we yield it to God to be used for His purpose.

Crossbills will show up wherever conifer cones are abundant, and they keep their twisted beaks busy. Are *you* using your God-given tool?

❖ Think about learning a new skill – it is never too late to develop a hidden talent.

Father, make me willing to use whatever tools You give me.

(CROSSBILL)

60
Blinding Pride

Read: 1 Peter 5:8-9
Key verse: Your adversary, the devil, prowls around like a roaring lion, seeking someone to devour.

Last week I was watching six male cardinals at my birdfeeders and delighting in their beauty against the green leaves of the spring trees. There was a sudden rush of gray feathers and an explosion of red birds frantically trying to escape a hawk. Before I could get to my feet, a cardinal was being carried off in the sharp talons of a sharp-shinned hawk. The beautiful scene had disintegrated, and I was saddened by the harsh reality of nature. I was also chagrined by the realization that the hawk will be back another day.

The cardinals were no doubt enjoying the lovely morning, taking time to eat while anticipating their spring work of nest building and raising their young. They weren't expecting an attack by a deadly enemy.

We too can become complacent and get caught off guard by Satan. We can be basking in our good deeds, our church work, our blessings – when suddenly we're in danger of getting caught and carried off. Not only is our enemy lurking about, he has an actual plan to entrap us; he knows when and where we are most vulnerable. He will show no mercy – and he will be back.

Sometimes we think we are above falling prey to sin, and that's the most dangerous situation of all. Pride can blind us to very large hawks.

❖ Ask yourself, *When and where am I most likely to be tempted?* Then avoid those situations.

> *Merciful God, open my eyes to see where I am most vulnerable. Forgive my foolish pride.*

61
Preparing for Hard Times

Read: Proverbs 6:4-9
Key verse: (The ant)…prepares her food in the summer.

Everyone knows that squirrels bury acorns in the fall, but we don't usually think of birds storing up food for the winter. However, many species hide seeds to increase their winter food supply. Woodpeckers, nuthatches, and members of the crow family habitually store food. The acorn woodpecker wedges nuts into holes it has made in the trunk of an oak tree or telephone pole. Eurasian nutcrackers bury nuts in caches in the ground, not only to eat during the winter, but also to feed young in the spring. The Grey jay, found in north Canadian forests, sticks insects and seeds into crannies with the help of its own saliva.

Being prepared for the future is a worthy goal for all of God's creatures. Solomon says in Proverbs 20:4 that the sluggard does not plow after the autumn, so he begs during the harvest and has nothing. Setting aside food (and money) is a sound practice – we are told to be good stewards and to be prepared for all kinds of emergencies, even if only to be able to help others. Many churches offer financial counseling for those who need help in balancing budgets or establishing a systematic savings plan.

But the most essential preparation is to have God's Word hidden in our hearts – to keep us from sinning, to help us be obedient, and to be ready for the perfect opportunity to share a kernel of truth.

❖ Prepare yourself for an emergency – store bottled water or an extra flashlight somewhere.

Father God, help me to memorize a morsel of scripture today.

62
Feeding the Hungry

Read: Luke 6:30-36
Key verse: Give to everyone who asks of you.

I saw a photo in a bird book of a male cardinal who frequently fed large goldfish in a pond in the birdwatcher's yard. The goldfish would swim to the edge of the pond and open their mouths. Then the cardinal, sitting on the edge of the pond, would drop food into them. We don't know why the cardinal did this – he just saw open mouths and felt the need to drop in food. We do know for sure that there's no way the fish would ever be able to feed the cardinal or repay him in any way.

In today's scripture lesson, we are told to give to anyone who begs of us – to be merciful and compassionate. We must not expect anything in return; in fact, we are told to be kind and loving to our enemies (who might just turn around and hurt us).

Jesus had great compassion for the poor and hungry. Matthew recorded the occasion when Jesus told His disciples to feed the multitude following Him because "I am not willing to send them away hungry" (Matt. 14:13-21). Jesus performed a miracle that day so that everyone could be fed.

It doesn't take a miracle for us to feed a hungry family – it takes only a willing heart.

❖ Look for some needy people in your area – contribute food where it is needed. Don't wait for Thanksgiving or Christmas.

Thank You, Lord, for my daily bread. Make me willing to share it.

63
Longing for Home

Read: Deuteronomy 30:1-5
Key verse: You return to the Lord your God.

For most of us, the words *going home* evoke warm feelings of happy memories with loved ones; we feel an emotional need to be with family. Even the famous movie alien E.T. pleaded to "phone home."

Scientists are still trying to understand how a bird's homing instinct works. One thing for certain is that a homing pigeon must have a firm attachment to its loft (permanent home where it was raised), and once the attachment has been established, it is extraordinarily difficult to train the pigeon to home to another spot. A highly trained pigeon will travel up to fifteen hundred miles in three days to go home.

There is a longing in the human spirit that makes us look for God and our heavenly home – even primitive cultures have a need to worship something or someone. But in our sophisticated surroundings, we attempt to fill that yearning with things such as relationships, materialism, and financial success. We may travel around the world, begin new hobbies, or start new careers; we may even experiment with drugs or the occult in our urgency to find a peace that makes us feel that our longing is fulfilled. What we all need to recognize is that this peace we long for is a peace that only God can give.

The Omnipotent Creator God is our "loft" – He has made all of us with a homing instinct to go to Him. Only in His presence are we truly home.

❖ Ask yourself if you are substituting things for God.

Father, thank You for Your constant call to come home to You.

64
A Hornbill's Wall

Read: Isaiah 26:1-4
Key verse: The steadfast of mind You will keep in perfect peace.

Hornbills are raucous birds found in Africa and Asia. They make their nests in large holes in trees. The female gets into the nest, and the male helps her make a wall of mud, leaving only a tiny slit just large enough to allow the male to feed her. She is then wholly dependent on him throughout egg-laying, incubation, and the earlier part of the nesting stage. The mother and her young are safe behind the wall, and they trust the male to take care of them. When the babies are two or three weeks old and start demanding more food than the father can provide, the mother breaks out of the nest in order to help feed the babies. The young then help wall themselves in again until they are full-grown, continuing to get fed by both parents.

God tells us we can trust Him to guard us – we can have perfect peace when we lean on Him. His salvation is our wall and bulwark. The Dead Sea Scrolls read, "You (Lord) have been to me a strong wall." In Him, we have the assurance that our minds and souls are safe not only here and now, but for all of eternity. Isaiah 60:18 says, "You will call your walls salvation." Our God not only saves us and feeds us, but He gives us the responsibility of feeding those who are hungry for His salvation.

❖ Share your faith with someone today, or sign up for a class on how to witness.

Almighty God, I praise You for Your strong wall of salvation.

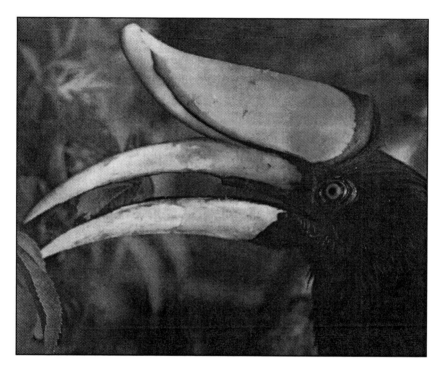

(HORNBILL)

65
Migration Mysteries

Read Psalm 139:1-12

Key verse: Where can I go from Your Spirit?

For thousands of years, men have marveled that birds disappear every fall, and then reappear in the spring. Aristotle thought swallows hibernated by submerging in swamps. A British scholar wrote in 1703 that birds passed the winter by journeying to the moon. Only recently have scientists used bird-banding, radar observations, and other studies to solve some of the mysteries of migration.

It is a marvelous truth that God not only knows the answers to our questions about migration, but He even knows where every bird in the world is at any given moment. He knows where *we* are and what *we* are doing, too. God is omniscient – He knows everything. He is also omnipresent – He is everywhere. Our minds simply cannot grasp this. We cannot hide from Him, we cannot deceive Him, and we cannot outsmart Him. All we can do is marvel as David did – "such knowledge is too wonderful for me." It's like lying on the lawn on a summer night, watching the stars and trying to understand the size of the universe.

A favorite children's book shows a pouting baby rabbit saying to his mother, "I'll become a bird and fly away from you." The mother replies, "I will be a tree that you come home to." God wants us to fly home to Him – that's where we belong.

❖ Read *The Runaway Bunny* to a child; talk about how God wants us to come to Him.

> *Almighty, all-knowing God, I want to be close to Your heart every day of my life.*

66
What Are You Saying?

Read: James 3:2-10
Key verse: From the same mouth come both blessing and cursing.

Ornithologists and poets have struggled for years to put into words what a bird's song sounds like. The Carolina wren supposedly says, "Teakettle, teakettle, teakettle, tea"; the cardinal sings, "What cheer, what cheer, birdie, birdie, birdie"; and the oven bird simply says, "Teacher, teacher." Some birds say happy things – the robin calls, "Cheer up, cheer up," while the peewee sighs, "Dear me, dear me." In the United States, the white-throated sparrow sings, "Old Sam Peabody, Peabody, Peabody" while our Canadian friends hear, "Oh, sweet Canada, Canada, Canada" from the identical bird. (Perhaps we hear what we want to hear.) And the mockingbird reports everything he hears all the other birds singing!

James tells us in today's reading how our tongues can be used to bless the Lord and then with the same mouth we curse men. He warns us the human tongue cannot be tamed – it is restless and evil.

When others listen to our speech, what do they hear – unkind words, gossip, cursing, foolishness? When we listen to other people, do we hear only what we want to hear? Are we like the mockingbird – repeating parts of conversations and constantly jabbering? Proverbs 21:33 says guarding our mouths and tongues keeps us from trouble. Wouldn't it be nice if we never needed to apologize for something we've said?

❖ Remember not to spoil an apology with an excuse.

Oh, God, I want my words and even my thoughts to sound like sweet music to Your ears.

67
A Hummingbird's Hard Work

Read: Proverbs 22:6
Key verse: Train up a child in the way he should go.

Both the male and female hummingbird work to build a nest, but it is only the female who does the actual construction. The ruby-throated female brings thistle and dandelion fuzz to a limb, and then glues the fuzz in place with pine resin and spider silk. A more flexible construction of plant fuzz and "glue" is used for walls, which the bird crimps by sitting in the nest and pinching the rim between her chin and her body. The outside of the nest is covered with bits of gray lichen. The male's responsibility is to provide protection of the area. He is fiercely territorial; if another male encroaches into the surroundings, there will be a fascinating aerial dogfight.

It takes a lot of patience, determination, and commitment on the part of both partners to build a hummingbird nest. Suppose the male were to get tired or bored with guarding the nesting site. What if the female decided to save time and energy by cutting back on the amount of spider silk she gathered? Or if she just skipped the lichen covering that helps to camouflage the nest?

It takes the same kind of fortitude to build a home and raise children today – two parents doing their best, fiercely determined to provide a safe, loving haven, and committed to bringing up those children in the way they should go. It isn't easy, especially for a single parent, but human parents have allies – family members, teachers, and the local church. It takes a Christian village to raise a Christian child today, and it starts with parents committed to God.

❖ Ask yourself if you need more patience, determination, or commitment in parenting. Then ask your pastor or a counselor for help, if necessary.

Thank You, Lord, for parents who are committed to You and to their families.

68
The Timing of Swallows

Read: Jeremiah 8:5-9

Key verse: The swallow and the crane observe the time of their return.

One of the best-known stories in bird lore is how the swallows arrive at Capistrano, California, every year on March 19. The birds have flown from Goya in Argentina, a distance of 8,200 miles, in exactly thirty days. Flying at 6,600 feet to take advantage of tail winds and to avoid predator birds, the swallows follow river valleys, mountains, and the coast of Baja California.

The birds are so dependable that every year on March 19 thousands of tourists arrive at the old Franciscan monastery of San Juan to celebrate the birds' safe journey. How do the swallows know on February 18 that it's the day to start the trip north? That's another one of God's secrets!

One of the things we know for certain about God is He is dependable. He keeps His promises, and His character never changes. 1 Corinthians 1:9 says God is faithful (refillable, trustworthy and therefore ever true to His promise, and He can be depended on) (AMP). God's timing is always perfect, not just in the migration of birds or the turning of the seasons, but even in our own lives. We usually aren't aware of it at the time, but when we look back, we can see how God worked things out in His time for our good.

❖ Make a list of situations in your life where God's timing has been perfect.

Almighty God, I am in awe of Your power and precision. Everything You do is perfect!

69
Binoculars to See God

Read: John 14:6-10
Key verse: He who has seen Me has seen the Father.

Anyone seriously interested in birdwatching knows how essential it is to have good binoculars. Even a bird you recognize in a nearby tree becomes much more interesting when viewed in detail. Colors are more vivid, the fieldmarks that identify birds are more obvious, and even small irregularities stand out. You can tell, for example, that the blue bird you see is not only a jay, but a scrubjay, and furthermore, it is the old scrubjay with the deformed foot that you saw last year! Professional birders use binoculars to observe bird behavior and then share their findings in books and magazines.

Jesus Christ is our "binoculars" to see God. Paul says in Colossians 1:15 that Jesus is the image of the invisible God. In Christ we see all of God's glory personified. We see God's characteristics – His love, grace, and compassion. We don't have to think of Him as a distant impersonal being – Jesus shows Him to us up-close and personal. In the Bible we learn not only what God is like, but how we can relate to Him. Jesus gives us the very words of God. Imagine binoculars that not only let us see a bird but also hear it!

❖ Write down ten things you know about God because you know His Son.

Thank You, Jesus, for coming to earth and putting a face on God.

(FLORIDA SCRUBJAY)

70
Sounding Like Christians

Read: John 15:1-7
Key verse: If you abide in Me, and My words abide in you.

In a poignant children's book by Taro Yashima, a young boy in Japan walks several miles through the mountains each day to attend school. His classmates discover on graduation day that Chibi has not only had perfect attendance through all the years, but he has learned to mimic the crows he has heard each day – newly hatched crows, mother and father crows, crows early in the morning, and even how crows cry when the village people have some unhappy accident. His imitations are so perfect that his classmates are awed and give him a new name: "Crow Boy."

If we are to sound like Christ – indeed, if we are to be called "Christians"– we will have to spend a lot of time with Him. We will need to know His words and how He spoke them. Was His voice loving or condemning when He spoke to the woman at the well? When the rich young ruler walked away from Jesus and His disciples, and Jesus said to them that it's hard for a rich man to enter heaven, were those words spoken in pity or anger? Not only what we say but how we say it is important when we want people to hear Christ in us.

In our busy lives, finding time to be quietly alone with the Lord, listening to His voice and studying His word, is crucial to our knowledge of Him and how He sounds.

❖ Ask yourself if you are so intimately acquainted with Jesus that you sound like Him.

Father, make me more like Jesus in what I say and how I say it.

71
Many Songs

Read: Psalm 92
Key verse: I will sing for joy at the works of Your hands.

One of the unanswered questions about bird song is why males of some species sing so many different songs. One theory is that a large repertoire signals to females that this singer is of a high status and quality. Another theory suggests that if he knows lots of songs, he is an older bird, and some female birds might prefer an experienced male to father her young.

But I prefer the "Beau Geste" theory. In the movie by the same name, a lone French Foreign Legionnaire defends a fort by propping up the bodies of his fellow soldiers and firing their guns. The attackers are fooled into believing the fort is heavily defended. When applied to the bird world, this theory proposes that one bird fools newly arriving males into believing the area is already densely occupied by many male birds. The newcomers are thus encouraged to move on.

It's not hard to understand why Christians sing so many songs. The great old hymns as well as the new praise choruses help us worship and pray, they bring comfort and healing, and they help us celebrate our oneness in Christ. Christian music lets us sing scripture, it reminds us of our heritage, and it gives us a tiny glimpse of what heaven will be like!

❖ Put a hymnal on your bathroom counter and sing a different song each morning or evening.

Father, I want to come into Your presence with singing today. May my joyful noise be pleasing to Your ears.

72
Danger!

Read: John 17:9-19
Key verse: The world has hated them.

The National Audubon Society is perhaps best known for its work in bird conservation. It concerns itself with all the factors that affect bird population – habitat quantity and quality, for example.

But there are other, more specific dangers for birds. Cats, foxes, and raccoons are among the most common predators in North America. Snakes, mice, and predatory birds also take large numbers of small birds and their eggs.

Diseases can profoundly affect bird populations; botulism and avian cholera can kill thousands of birds in one outbreak. Other factors such as weather and fire can influence the numbers of birds, either directly or by affecting the food supply or habitat.

Unfortunately, there are many factors that negatively impact Christian populations around the world. Persecution and martyrdom have become common in some countries, and modern cults have caused confusion among many young people. Some Christians are lulled into ineffectiveness by busy schedules, wrong priorities, and just plain laziness. The world urges us to compromise our values and water down the truth of the gospel. Now, more than ever, the universal Christian church needs to be involved in Christian conservation and preservation.

❖ Pray daily for Christians in dangerous places.

Don't let me be a passive Christian, Lord. Help me be alert to all the danger around me.

73
Pecking Orders

Read: James 2:1-9
Key verse: **If you show partiality, you are committing sin.**

Most corporations have a "pecking order." The new employee quickly learns who ranks above and below him or her, and adjusts his or her behavior accordingly. Even in schools, there is a kind of pecking order (and the person with the most clout is often the custodian!). Families may have a certain pecking order, too – have you seen the bumper sticker that says, "If mama ain't happy, ain't nobody happy"?

Social birds follow a behavioral pattern known as the "peck order." This refers to a hierarchy with a bold, forceful leader and a long line of underlings arranged by rank from general down to private, each with certain privileges. Thus, "Big Birds" can peck at or threaten "Little Birds," taking their food and even pulling out their feathers. Quarrels are usually within a flock and don't involve outsiders. The pecking order can also be flexible – a bird can be dominant in certain conditions and times of the year and not others. There is also the possibility of "marrying" to achieve social status – a dominant male cardinal's mate will have the same status that he does in the flock.

I'm thankful God has no pecking order. He loves us all the same, and Peter reminds us that with God, there is no partiality: "God plays no favorites! It makes no difference who you are or where you're from" (Acts 10:34) (TMB). There is no place in the church for a pecking order, either. As Christ's disciples, we need to remember that there are no "Big Birds" or "Little Birds." We all have a role to play, we are all important, and we all deserve respect.

❖ Examine your attitude toward fellow Christians. Are you guilty of snobbery?

Father, give me humility and a servant's heart.

74
Cheating Chickadees

Read: Malachi 2:13-17

Key verse: Keep a watch upon your spirit that you deal not treacherously and faithlessly with your marriage mate. (AMP)

A Canadian scientist recently published a fascinating study about female chickadees and their lack of faithfulness to their mates. Male chickadees are constantly challenged to a song contest with rival males, and the females listen to determine who is winning. If her mate loses, the female sneaks away and cheats on her mate. It was proven by DNA that one or two babies in her nest had a different father than the one who raised them.

We are tempted to chuckle over this tidbit of information, but it is sobering to think people are frequently just as shallow. We have all heard stories of hearts and homes broken because one spouse wanted someone better looking, younger, or richer. It's especially sad to see a spouse leaving because his or her mate has Alzheimer's disease or another debilitating condition.

God hates divorce, He hates adultery, and He hates the attitude that says, "I want my own happiness and I don't care who gets hurt." But God still loves the people who commit these sins, and He offers them forgiveness and healing.

"Your Cheatin' Chickadee Heart" sounds like a country-music classic; a better song for the Christian to sing might be "I Would Be True."

❖ Repeat your wedding vows with your spouse, or determine to be faithful to your friends.

Lord, thank You for Your faithfulness and Your promise never to leave me or forsake me.

75
Working at Molting

Read: Psalm 80:1-7
Key verse: O God, restore us.

Healthy feathers are essential to a bird's existence, so birds regularly replace their feathers in the process called molt. The feathers are dropped in a regular sequence at certain times of the year. It is a slow process, with replacement taking place at a pace that keeps up with losses. In this way, the bird is never without feathers. Some ornithologists suggest birds are under stress during the molt period and seek relief through extra drinking and bathing. All adult birds molt at least once annually. Growing new feathers takes a lot of energy, so molt usually takes place after the young have been raised or after the fall migration.

It is important for us as Christians to keep ourselves renewed as well, except ours is an inward renewal. Not only do we need to molt off unhealthy attitudes and ugly habits, we need to grow more fruits of the Spirit – patience, goodness, and kindness, for example. A bird doesn't have to think about molting – it just happens automatically. But we have to work at shedding undesirable traits and then developing positive ones. We must cooperate with the Holy Spirit within us, and that might mean going to Bible studies, praying with a group or prayer partner, attending church regularly, even "migrating" to a weekend retreat occasionally. We need to be at our very best – in peak condition spiritually – if we are to be effective in our Christian work.

❖ Give yourself a spiritual vitamin – take a day off for quality time with God.

Father, when I'm feeling drab and ineffective, renew my heart's passion for You.

76
Who's Helping the Babies?

Read: 1 Thessalonians 3:1-10
Key verse: And we sent Timothy…to strengthen and establish and to exhort and comfort and encourage you in your faith.

The apostlebird is found only in Australia and is remarkable for its social qualities. The members of a group stay together all year round. They all help build the nest and share in incubation. The whole family will line up to present food to the nestlings, and there even can be competition over who will be next to help the babies. But there's an ironic twist to the story. Despite all the helpers and despite starting out with a large clutch of eggs, it is very rare for more than three nestlings to be raised, and they generally leave the nest before they can fly properly.

Is there a lesson here for those of us concerned with discipling baby Christians? We may all rejoice when someone comes to Christ, but who will be responsible for mentoring and nourishing that new believer? Or what about the new family who visits your church? Even if many people greet the newcomers, but nobody invites them to Sunday school or a Bible study, they may not come back or get involved.

As a teacher, I was always concerned that a child could "drop through the cracks" and not get individual help if needed. As Christians, we should be ready to come along side of anyone who needs loving care and to be there until they can "fly properly."

❖ Ask your pastor how you could care for or mentor new people in your church.

Father, help me want to be personally committed to those who need extra care.

(APOSTLEBIRD)

77
Leaving the Nest

Read: Philippians 3:12-16
Key verse:...not that I have now attained this ideal. (AMP)

Baby birds are called "precocial young" when they are hatched with feathers or down and can leave the nest soon after hatching. Birds that nest on the ground are usually precocial, such as killdeer, pheasants, and waterfowl.

In contrast, nestlings that are almost helpless are known as "altricial young." They are naked with closed eyes and must depend on their parents for food and warmth. Groups with altricial young include songbirds, woodpeckers, and hummingbirds.

Young birds are usually brooded (kept warm) until they can regulate their body temperature; even many precocial young need to be brooded, especially during bad weather.

In today's reading, Paul gives us a formula for growth in our Christian walk. And even this great apostle admits he's not where he wants to be in his spiritual growth. Some of us start out in Christian homes, singing "Jesus Loves Me" when we're tots. Some of us, however, have to struggle in our early faithwalk; we may need lots of encouragement. Two things are certain: we *all* must accept Jesus as our own personal Savior, and we *all* need to keep on growing spiritually. Ephesians 4:13 points out that we are not fully mature until we have reached the fullness and completeness found in Christ. Just when I'm feeling pretty good about myself, I realize I'm barely out of the nest!

❖ Ask God to point out where you need to grow. Write down at least one area that He shows you.

Father, I long to be a mature Christian. Make me willing to do whatever it takes.

78
Lulled into Conforming

Read: Romans 12:1-2

Key verse: Don't become so well-adjusted to your culture that you fit into it without even thinking. (TMB)

The ultimate thrill for many birders is having a wild bird sit in their hand or perch on their shoulder. Achieving this close encounter doesn't take any great skill or luck, but it does require patience. Birds can be trained to lose their fear of people. You can purchase a cardboard cut-out of a person with an outstretched hand holding seeds. Once birds start eating from the cardboard hand, you can dress like the fake person – put a similar cap on your head, wear the same color clothing, hold out your hand with seeds – and birds who had become accustomed to the cardboard person will eat from your hand. The birds have been lulled into a sense of normalcy and safety.

Can this happen to Christians? There is evil all around us, but it can be camouflaged until we slowly become accustomed to it. Several years ago I went to a play with friends. As we left the theater, I chuckled over the play's humor. Then I realized I was laughing about blatant adultery. I had been drawn into the plot so thoroughly that the adultery seemed normal – not only permissible, but even a good thing. Many things considered sinful fifty years ago are now accepted – the change occurred so subtly we weren't aware the standards had shifted.

God warns us not to conform to this world; He wants us to be salt and light – to stand out and make a difference.

❖ Make a list of areas where you're on the edge of conforming.

Give me the courage, God, to be firm in my convictions.

79
Camouflage Protection

Read: Psalm 18:30-33
Key verse: He is a shield to all who take refuge in Him.

When my daughters were young, they complained that mother birds were drab and plain compared to the fathers; they thought God wasn't being fair to the females. I told them God wanted to protect the females, especially when they were sitting on nests.

The truth is, though, most birds – male *or* female – do have some kind of camouflage. Owls can hardly be seen when sitting in a tree. The female meadowlark blends in with the grasses and dry leaves on the ground where she nests. Killdeer have special protection: the birds as well as their eggs look so much like pebbles that it's very hard to see them on the edge of a gravel road.

God is not only concerned about protecting our physical lives, He provides for our spiritual safety as well. The Bible tells us that when temptations come, God provides a way for escape. We can resist temptation by remembering scripture: "Thy word have I hid in my heart that I might not sin against Thee" (Ps. 119:11 KJV). We are told to be alert for temptation and to flee from it.

God provides all kinds of protection; it's our responsibility to use it.

❖ Read all of Psalm 18.

Father, thank You for Your hand of protection on my body as well as my soul.

(KILLDEER)

80
Sleep Tight!

Read: Proverbs 3:24-27
Key verse: When you lie down, you will not be afraid.

When it's dark outside and all the birds have left the feeders and yards, I wonder where they are sleeping. Sometimes I startle a bird roosting in a hanging basket if I go out to water my flowers, and I have seen other birds sleeping under the eaves or on door ledges. The bird books say most birds simply find sheltered spots – in tree cavities, empty birdhouses, or special nests made just for roosting. The most common sleeping position is not with their heads under their wings, but with the head turned and resting on the back. Only the bill is tucked under feathers. Birds are also known to nap – closing their eyes and sleeping for a few minutes in the midst of feeding or other activities.

Some birds roost in groups, which is a benefit in the winter because they keep each other warm. Communal roosts also provide increased safety since there nearly always will be a few birds awake at any moment to give the alarm if needed.

I have never liked being alone at night – I much prefer "communal roosting." If I have to sleep in an empty house, I tend to keep one eye open. Then I'm ashamed when I think of all the little birds that simply squat down over their feet and close their eyes – not looking or listening for scary things. If God keeps me safe in the daytime, why would He forget about me in the dark?

Psalm 121:3 reminds us that God does not sleep; in fact, He is even thinking about us as *we* sleep. I like the little plaque that says we should give our troubles to God when we go to bed, because He's going to be up all night anyway.

❖ Memorize the old hymn "Wonderful Peace" and sing it as your personal lullaby.

Forgive me, Lord, for letting fear creep into my head at night.

81
Imprinting on Jesus

Read: Ephesians 4:1-3, 17-26
Key verse: And put on the new self.

Many interesting studies have been done on imprinting – a phenomenon that occurs when a young bird (or animal) forms a strong attachment and identification with its caretaker. Animals that imprint on humans do not behave appropriately, and usually cannot survive in their natural habitat. To prevent this, ornithologists who raise baby cranes will dress up in crane costumes when teaching the colts (baby cranes) to search for food. This is important, because once a crane imprints, it cannot be retrained to act like a bird. The young birds must also be taught to have a healthy fear of people.

Christians are to imprint Jesus. We should form such a strong identification with Him that we don't act like worldly people. Paul says in today's reading that we must lead a life worthy of our divine calling. If we have been taught by Christ, we will strip ourselves of our former nature and put on the new nature created in God's image. We won't just *act* like Christ; we will actually have His nature. We must be a new and different person, holy and good.

If we are imprinted on Jesus, our behavior should identify us as Christians; we know that we belong to Him. We are free from our old nature; we can't say, "The devil made me do it." When we sin, it's usually because we choose to do so.

❖ Find and learn the old hymn "I Would Be Like Jesus."

Lord Jesus, help me to imprint on You. I want to have Your nature.

82
Mobbing the Enemy

Read: 2 Chronicles 32:1-8

Key verse: But with us is the Lord our God to help us and to fight our battles.

One summer I watched with amusement as a mockingbird dive-bombed our neighbor's cat almost daily as it strolled down the sidewalk. This behavior, called mobbing, occurs when one or more birds attack an enemy – an owl, snake, or other predator. Mobbing involves some risk to the mobber; some birds rarely lead the charge but may fly along with the group.

It is interesting that two of the most tenacious and aggressive songbirds in mobbing activities are the little chickadee and its cousin, the titmouse. They are small but mighty when a small owl is located. They not only will scold the predator but actually will strike the enemy from behind.

It takes courage to attack an adversary, especially if it is bigger than you or if you have nobody to help you. In today's reading, Hezekiah reminded the Jewish people that their enemies only had arms of flesh, but Israel's God was greater than all their enemies and He would help them.

What adversary are you facing? Has a deadly disease struck you or a loved one? Is there a mountainous problem in your home? Whatever the battle, first make sure God is on your side – and He is if you have a personal relationship with Him through Christ. Then get some other "mobbers" to be prayer warriors with you.

❖ Memorize Isaiah 41:13.

Thank You, God, for promising to help me. Help me remember that You are greater than my problems.

83
Migration Problems

Read: 2 Timothy 4:1-8
Key verse: But you, be sober in all things, endure hardship.

One of the marvels of bird migration is that such small creatures can travel so far, so quickly, and so accurately. Of course, not every bird that starts out arrives safely, and some birds don't land when or where they expected. There are several factors that can hinder migration.

Probably the greatest hindrance is bad weather. Rain and fog can interfere with the bird's use of visible landmarks such as rivers or shorelines. Strong winds can blow small birds off course, and severe cold spells coming sooner than usual can wreak havoc. Even a heat wave can make some birds stop flying.

Birds that cross the ocean need to be well-fueled before starting out, and they need to find food quickly when they arrive on land. If there is a famine on either end, a bird may not survive.

Unfortunately, there can be hindrances in our Christian journey as well. Lack of solid biblical teaching weakens us and leaves us vulnerable. We starve spiritually if we don't read our Bibles. We need fellow Christians around us to share their faith and pray with us. Satan, of course, does everything he can to discourage us. Fatigue, worry, and stress can drag us down and get us off course. But if we keep focused on Jesus we will be able to say with Paul, "I have kept the faith" (2 Tim. 4:7).

❖ Pray over the telephone frequently with a Christian friend.

Lord God, give me wisdom and strength to overcome the hindrances in my walk with You.

84
Enslaved Ospreys

Read: 2 Peter 2:17-20
Key verse: For by what a man is overcome, by this he is enslaved.

The osprey, a large fish-eating bird of prey, is found throughout most of the world. Called a fish hawk in North America, it will also eat small mammals and birds. The osprey cruises above the water at heights up to two hundred feet, and dives when it spots a fish. Frequently submerging completely, the bird can catch a fish as deep as three feet in the water. The osprey's sharp talons clutch the fish, which is then carried back to a tree or the nest. But there's a problem: sometimes the fish is too big to carry, and the osprey is unable to let go. One theory is the excitement of the catch stimulates a locking mechanism – the bird is unable to release the fish. Some people believe the claws simply sink into bone and get stuck. Fishermen have caught large fish with osprey feet still attached. Unfortunately, the feature that helps the osprey can also lead to its death.

The same problem can also trap people. Someone with a little skill or luck at gambling can quickly become addicted and unable to quit, even when it becomes apparent that the gambler could lose his or her job, home, and family. I know a woman who couldn't resist using her credit card – a helpful tool that most of us use regularly. But it became a dangerous luxury for her, and eventually led to her losing everything in bankruptcy. The desire to make money quickly can lure a businessperson into shady deals, and then when he or she wants out, it's too late. We need to be very careful not to sink our "talons" into something we can't release. We can be pulled under and lose everything we cherish.

❖ Examine your habits and pastimes. Is there anything you couldn't let go of if you needed or wanted to?

> *Father, give me wisdom regarding anything that might entrap me. Give me the strength to break away if necessary.*

(OSPREY)

85
Firm Commitment

Read: Proverbs 9:7-12
Key verse: If you are wise, you are wise for yourself.

A biologist in Quebec has discovered that some female birds select their mates by copying choices of other females rather than using their own judgment. The research indicates these females somehow judge their own assessment to be flawed, and younger birds especially might tend to copy the criteria used by older females. But even as those uncertain females age, they still tend to doubt themselves.

Getting good counsel is one thing, but letting other people influence our choices is another. It's easy to be swayed into poor decisions when we have no confidence in ourselves. Paul told the Romans that each man should be fully convinced in his own mind, and he urged Timothy not to feel inferior just because he was young. We need to know what we believe and why we believe it, otherwise we can be confused by scoffers or easily led astray.

When we have an important decision to make, we should first pray about it and ask other Christians to be praying. Then we gather all the information that is pertinent to the decision, we read our Bibles to see if there are specific directions on that topic, and we talk to our pastors or trusted advisors.

We sometimes wonder why people don't learn from their mistakes. The female birds who copied others seemed to persist in that pattern. But we Christians have a Helper, and He is at work in us to give us boldness in our convictions.

❖ Write down ten spiritual truths on which you cannot be shaken.

> *Father, I know whom I have believed and am persuaded that You are able to keep that which I've committed unto You against that day!* (2 Tim. 1:12 KJV)

86
Admirable Blue Jays

Read: Philippians 4:4-9

Key verse: If there is any excellence and if anything worthy of praise, dwell on these things.

Most birdwatchers are hard pressed to say something nice about blue jays. Except for being beautiful, they aren't a pleasure to have at your feeder – they're greedy, noisy, and will eat the eggs of songbirds. But if you study jays, you can find a few admirable qualities. Blue jays will keep a predator in view and often attempt to drive it away – they are the watch dogs around the feeder.

Some folks grudgingly admit the blue jay is honest when he calls out, "Thief" because he is accurately announcing his arrival at the feeder! So there you have it – some admirable traits of blue jays.

Why is it that we usually prefer to find bad traits of people rather than look for the good? Do we feel better about our own shortcomings? My mother used to remind me if I couldn't say something good about another person, not to say anything at all. Christians especially should assume responsibility not only for building each other up, but for protecting each other when being verbally attacked. And it can be done without any confrontation. If something negative is said, then gently say something positive you have observed about that person, even if (and this is important) you aren't particularly fond of that person. It isn't easy, but it can be done.

❖ Find good traits about others so you're ready to praise them – either to their face or behind their back to other people.

Lord, I'm going to need Your help – and Your love – to do this. Give me the mind of Christ, who sees potential in all of us.

87
Loon Blessings

Read: Jeremiah 29:10-14
Key verse: For I know the plans I have for you.

When my husband and I visited Maine a few summers ago, I was eager to hear my first loon. I always had wanted to hear first hand that hauntingly beautiful cry I had heard only on soundtracks. So one evening after dinner we drove out of town to a large lake, sat at a picnic table, and looked out over the water. We never did hear a loon, but God thrilled our hearts with a blessing different from what we had expected and hoped for. As we watched, a spectacular sunset began to form, and we took several photographs we still treasure.

Life sometimes goes that way. Doors close on career choices, people walk out of our lives, and dreams have to be abandoned. We question why, we say life isn't fair, and we may even get angry at God. But when we back up and look again – perhaps with the passing of time and the use of a different lens, we see the blessing God was unfolding. The longer we walk with the Lord, the more we see His hand on our lives, and the more willing we are to accept His choice of blessings.

I finally heard my loon – four years later on a lake in Wisconsin. There are still some sounds I'd like to hear – or things I'd like to accomplish – but I'm grateful for the way God leads me and for the unexpected blessings He gives me.

❖ Make a list of ways God has surprised you with blessings.

You know best, Lord. Help me to see Your hand on my life. Thank You, God, for unexpected blessings.

(COMMON LOON)

88
Unreasonable Demands

Read: Job 40:1-5
Key verse: What can I reply to You?

In a beautifully illustrated children's book, an inchworm gladly measures parts of birds' bodies – the heron's leg, the toucan's beak, the flamingo's neck – and the whole hummingbird! But the nightingale demands, "Measure my song, or I'll eat you for breakfast."

The nightingale's unreasonable threat makes me wonder about some of my requests of God. Do I say, "Lord, make me rich so I can live like my neighbor"? Or is my most fervent prayer for my children to be happy, even though I have learned character is built in adversity. I know of a woman who nearly demanded God give her daughter a sunny day for her wedding, and then when it poured all day, the woman's faith wavered a bit.

We need to examine our attitude as well as our words when we pray. God has said we can come boldly to His throne – we don't have to cower in fear. Our God is approachable because Christ is our advocate. But we must make our requests humbly, remembering that God knows what is best for us – He sees the whole picture. Jesus teaches us in the Lord's Prayer to ask simply for God's will to be done (Matt. 6:10).

❖ Say the Lord's Prayer slowly and see why it is a model prayer for us.

Father God, forgive me for my foolish demands. Help me, Holy Spirit, to pray as I ought.

89
Ugly Garbage

Read: 1 John 1:6-10
Key verse: If we say that we have no sin, we are deceiving ourselves.

Anyone who watches birds for any length of time will see a parent bird bring food to the nest and then leave with a small, white object – the ornithological equivalent of a messy diaper! This fecal sac is a mucous membrane in which feces of baby birds are wrapped. To keep the nest clean, clear of parasites, and free from smells that may attract predators, the adult bird will dispose of the sac well away from the nest. Most backyard birds' nests are amazingly clean when the babies have fledged.

Is there a lesson here for us? Not only should we keep our homes free from garbage such as pornography and vulgar music, but more importantly we need to check our personal lives for those things that make us unattractive or even repulsive. How about our language? Have we become careless with profanity or crude expressions? Do we have habits that are a poor witness of our Christian walk? How about attitudes?

When my daughters were teenagers, I had to remind them frequently to clean up their rooms, but it was a serious matter when I told them they needed to clean up their acts. Allowing the Holy Spirit to cleanse us inwardly is of eternal importance. There's no time like the present to get rid of ugly garbage in our lives!

❖ Do some serious cleaning – get rid of anything about which the Holy Spirit is nudging you.

> *Oh, God, I need Your help – not only to see the dirt in my life but then to have the determination to remove it.*

90
Crucial Decisions

Read: Ruth 1:8-18
Key verse: Where you lodge, I will lodge.

Downy woodpeckers usually lead separate lives in fall and early winter. A pair may remain on the same territory, but they will not feed together. Then in late winter, both the male and female begin drumming on their separate drumming posts. The drumming keeps the pair in closer touch with each other. Over the next three months, the pair increasingly synchronizes their activities. A crucial point in their lives comes when they choose a tree for their nest hole. If the pair cannot agree on a site, they may go their separate ways; if they can agree, the nest becomes the center of all their activities until the young birds fledge (leave the nest).

In today's scripture reading, Ruth had a crucial decision to make – a decision that would affect not only her life but all future generations. Although Naomi suggested Ruth should go her own way, Ruth made the decision to make her home with Naomi, and nothing could make her change her mind.

Many people stay on the fringes of Christianity, and they may even synchronize their activities with the church. But when the critical point comes – when Christ asks them to make a serious commitment to Him, to take up their cross and follow Him – they tell Him goodbye. And, sadly, future generations can be affected.

❖ If you never have made a commitment to follow Christ, do it right now.

Lord Jesus, I want to be with You for eternity. Come into my life and make my heart Your home.

91
Dangerous Decoys

Read: 2 Timothy 3:12-17
Key verse: Evil men and imposters will proceed from bad to worse, deceiving and being deceived.

I was amazed recently when I spotted an owl on a farmer's high TV antenna. It was only after seeing it three successive days that I realized it was fake – probably placed there to keep blackbirds off the antenna.

Sometimes decoys are used to attract birds rather than frighten them away. A hunter trying to lure geese to a field will set out decoys to attract overhead geese to land there. The geese assume the field is safe, especially when the decoys are positioned the way real geese would stand. Decoys are frequently successful, because geese, like people, are gullible and can be duped into believing what their eyes tell them. Just because something resembles the real thing does not mean it's genuine; it can, in fact, be dangerous.

Cults are like decoys. They lure unsuspecting people away from the truth of God's Word. Most cults resemble Christianity in some way and can be very appealing, especially to young people. But when closely examined in the light of the Bible, errors and discrepancies become glaring. People don't like to admit they were gullible, so it is hard for them to break away. But it's dangerous to stay, because cults, like hunters, usually have ulterior motives. Jesus said if we continued in His word, we would know the truth and the truth would make us free (John 8:32).

❖ Know the Bible so well that you can recognize a counterfeit religion. Sign up for a Bible study soon.

Lord Jesus, give me wisdom and discernment. I want to know the truth.

92
Skimming Off the Top

Read: Hebrews 5:12-14
Key verse: For everyone who partakes only of milk is not accustomed to the word of righteousness, for he is an infant.

The black skimmer is a water bird that forages for small fish swimming near the water's surface. This method relies entirely on chance contact with the fish. Skimmers forage mainly at night on calm waters. When the lower bill (which is longer than the upper one) makes contact with a small fish, the bird's head snaps downward and the prey is gripped, tossed up, and gulped down.

The skimmer makes me think of people who are "skimmers" of Christianity. They think dipping into church a few times a year is sufficient. Or perhaps they attend church faithfully, but skim through the Bible – maybe even reading it through each year, but never studying it or applying it to their lives. Then there are those who sit in their pews for years, skimming off the top what is offered by the church's ministries, but never getting involved. (These are the ones who sometimes say they get nothing out of the service.)

Skimming doesn't usually make for a well-nourished, growing Christian. Relying on chance encounters with God can lead to spiritual starvation. We need to have a well-planned, consistent, in-depth program for our spiritual health.

❖ Write down your plan for growing spiritually. Include short-term as well as long-term goals.

> *Forgive me, God, for skimming when I could be feasting on all that You offer me.*

(BLACK SKIMMER)

93
Meadowlark Distinction

Read: Matthew 26:69-75
Key verse: Even the way you talk gives you away.

It is extremely difficult to distinguish between western and eastern meadowlarks. (Geography doesn't help much; the birds overlap territories.) Both species are heavy-bodied, short-tailed, and long-billed. Plumage differences are subtle – the birds look alike. Both birds are found in open, grassy habitats, often perching on fences or fence posts. The most reliable clue in identification is probably their voices. The eastern meadowlark's song is higher and clearer than the western, and the eastern male sings fifty to one hundred songs, while the western sings fewer than ten. Extended listening is necessary to identify which bird you are hearing.

Our speech is often a clue to our spirituality. There is usually a big difference between the words of committed Christians and those who are totally indifferent to things of God. The Christian avoids swearing, vulgar jokes, racial slurs, and gossip. But Christians can be careless in their speech by using God's names irreverently. I cringe when I hear God referred to as "the man upstairs" or "the guy in the sky." I know many good, moral people whose speech offers nothing negative, but you don't hear them using phrases like "I thank God for…" or "The Lord has been teaching me…"

What does your speech say about you? Are you easily identified as a Christian?

❖ Do a speech check today. What are you saying – or not saying?

Holy Spirit, help me monitor my words. I want to be readily identified as a follower of Christ.

94
Nitpicking Nuisances

Read: 1 Thessalonians 5:9-15
Key verse: Live in peace with one another.

Many people dislike house sparrows and consider them nuisances. Farmers don't like them because they congregate in grain sheds, eating and fouling the grain. Homeowners don't like them because they build messy nests in just about any crevice or hole. Songbird fans are angry with sparrows because they don't sing, and they take over nesting spots of birds that do. I was amused to read of yet another unlovable quality of sparrows – they enjoy squabbling over nothing. In this particular incident, one sparrow was simply pecking at a little patch of snow on a limb, and soon the rest of the flock began shouldering and pecking at each other in a furious attempt to get at the snow – as though it were the last snow on earth.

I was reminded of Euodia and Syntyche, the two quarreling women admonished by Paul (Phil. 4:2). These women had shared in Paul's struggle to preach the gospel, so it could not have been a major issue they were debating. Perhaps it was nothing more than which one of them would be Paul's hostess when he got out of jail. Unfortunately, women can really get caught up in details about which men couldn't care less! We can become like a flock of sparrows – flitting, nitpicking, pecking at each other, and making general nuisances of ourselves. Paul went on to urge the Philippians to have forbearing spirits – an impossible assignment for sparrows, but certainly not for godly people who want to honor Christ.

❖ Make the effort to be a peacemaker in your church.

> *Lord, I want to be a woman (or man) of excellence. Keep me from being a nitpicking nuisance.*

95
Looks Are Deceiving

Read: 1 Kings 3:6-14
Key verse: So give thy servant an understanding heart to judge Your people to discern good and evil.

The mute swan was introduced to North America from Eurasia and now lives here in temperate areas. It is a beautiful bird, admired for its regal poise and snow-white plumage. But since mute swans are not native birds, biologists are concerned about their effect on native species. They can be very aggressive, and they also feed voraciously on aquatic plants. As populations of mute swans increase, they may out-compete smaller water birds for food. To complicate matters, they live a long time – up to twenty-six years.

There are many things in life that look beautiful to us on the surface, but after careful scrutiny, we see flaws. The Hollywood lifestyle may appear to be glamorous, but it ruins many lives. We may envy our neighbor's magnificent home and luxury cars, not realizing those things are causing the owner to be deeply in debt and perhaps creating a family crisis. There are even some religions that appear to have all the answers, but are far from the truth of God's Word. Remember that Satan made the apple look beautiful to Eve! We need to examine those things in our lives that appeal to us because of their beauty or apparent perfection. Looks truly can be deceiving.

❖ Look beneath the surface at your list of "wants" or goals. Might a problem be lurking?

> *Like Solomon, Father, I pray for wisdom. Help me discern what is best for me.*

(MUTE SWAN)

96
Seagulls or Christians

Read: Acts 11:19-30

Key verse: The disciples were first called Christians in Antioch.

Scientifically, there is no such species as "seagull," and some dictionaries don't include the word. However, it is very commonly used as a catch-all name for the many different kinds of gulls such as laughing gulls, herring gulls, and black-backed gulls. (The story is told of an old professor asked by a student about "seagulls." He scratched his head, then replied, "I don't know about C-gulls or D-gulls, but the E-gull is our national bird.") A serious ornithologist does not lump birds together. Each bird is identified by class, family, order, genus, species, subfamilies, and subspecies.

On the other hand, I think God lumps together all of us who follow Christ – He calls us *Christians*. It will not matter at the door of heaven if we call ourselves Lutherans, Methodists, Catholics, or Presbyterians. There will be only one classification in heaven: those who accepted Jesus Christ as Savior. People who just assume they are Christians because they're not Hindus or Muslims – or because they were brought up in a Christian home – need to check their status. We are Christians if we're in the family of God, and we join that family only by acknowledging that Jesus died for our personal sins.

❖ Make sure you have the right credentials for heaven.

Heavenly Father, I know I have sinned, and I do believe Jesus died for me. Make me Your child and change me into the kind of person I should be.

97
Accidents?

Read: Deuteronomy 32:1-4
Key verse: His work is perfect, for all His ways are just.

While reading a bird book recently I was intrigued by the term *accidental species*. This refers to birds found in locations other than their usual habitat. For example, three kinds of buntings that breed in eastern Asia have been spotted in Alaska in the spring. These birds were probably blown off course by storms while migrating. Great Frigatebirds nest in tropical oceans, but sightings in Oklahoma have been recorded. Other birds are considered accidental if they escape from a pet shop and then live on their own. (To be considered "regular," a species must occur at least ten times within twenty-five years).

I'm thankful that in God's kingdom there really are no "accidents." Every human being has worth – even before birth. God has a plan for every life, and we are all precious in His sight.

It is also no accident that we are born when we are and where we are. God does not make mistakes. Revelation 15:3 says, "Great and marvelous are Thy works, Oh Lord God, the Almighty."

❖ Sing "How Great Thou Art" to praise God today.

> *I thank You, Lord, that I am special to You. Help me to remember that every life is important – You've never had an accident.*

131

98
Hold On and Be Still

Read: Deuteronomy 33:26-29
Key verse: Underneath are the everlasting arms.

The moorhen (also called the common gallinule) is a water bird related to cranes. Found on every continent, it is part of a very large family. But because it lives in remote – usually marshy – areas, little is known about moorhens. One interesting characteristic, however, has been observed and recorded. It has to do with the moorhen's hiding technique. When danger threatens, the moorhen slips into nearby water, submerges, and then retains its position in the water by holding onto underwater vegetation with its feet. The bird then waits quietly for the enemy to leave.

People frequently need something to hang onto. The old joke about tying a knot in your rope and hanging on isn't much help if you don't have a rope in the first place. As Christians, we know God is our deep, underlying source of strength and safety. Even though we cannot see Him, He is there when we reach for Him. Psalm 46 reminds us God is our refuge and strength, a very present help in trouble. The psalmist goes on to say be still – stand silent – and know "that I am God." The moorhen knows instinctively to hold on and be still; we human beings have to learn that lesson, and it's very difficult – especially when we are forced to learn it in times of crisis. God wants us to be prepared for such times. His Word assures us He will never leave us to flounder.

❖ Read Psalm 46. Write down the part most meaningful to you.

Oh, God, when I feel like I'm drowning in sorrow or pain, help me to hang on to You.

(MOORHEN)

99
Listening to Angels

Read: Luke 12:54-57
Key verse: You do not know how to discern.

Many years ago in a radio commercial advertising a detergent called "Rinso," a woman's voice mimicked a quail saying, "Rinso White, Rinso White!" When I was five years old (and familiar with the commercial), I ran into my house one day and announced to my mother that out in the field an angel was singing, "Rinso White." Never having heard a quail before, I was certain I was hearing an angel.

In the clamor of all the world's voices, we need discernment to know when God is speaking and what He is saying to us. The basic truth in recognizing God's voice is this: He never will tell us something contrary to His written words. I know a woman who felt God was telling her to leave her husband so she could devote more time to God's work. God would not contradict what He says in the Bible about valid reasons for divorce.

God doesn't always "sound" the way we think He should. Elijah expected God to speak in the wind, an earthquake, and a fire. What Elijah finally heard was a still, small voice (1 Kings 19:11-13). Sometimes we have to be listening really hard to hear God, and that might involve digging into His word, fervently praying, and listening to wise counsel. God knows when we *truly* want to hear Him. Jesus said, "Be careful how you listen, for to him who has (spiritual knowledge), more will be given" (Luke 8:18 AMP).

❖ Determine to tune out confusing worldly voices – stop listening to things you know aren't spiritually healthy for you.

Father, help me to be discerning in my listening.

100
"Happily Ever After"

Read: 2 Corinthians 5:16-21
Key verse: We don't evaluate people by what they have or how they look. (TMB)

Hans Christian Andersen's beautiful tale of the ugly duckling strikes a chord in almost everyone. Who of us has not felt ugly, stupid, or unloved at some point in our lives? As a former teacher, I know that children who feel ugly sometimes act out in ugly ways. Teens who have been teased sometimes resort to violence, and some adults lash out in their workplace or perhaps sink into depression when told they are no longer needed. Real-life stories don't always end with "happily ever after."

Have you ever looked at someone with consistently ugly behaviors and wondered how that person would look or behave if he were a Christian? Paul tells us in today's reading that when we accept Christ we become a brand new creation – the old life with its attitudes, actions, and habits passes away. A new life begins!

Christians are not always beautiful in their actions, but as they allow the Holy Spirit to control them, they become more and more attractive to others. Ugly ducklings *can* become swans, and the Christian's life *will* end with "happily ever after."

❖ Try to see yourself and others as God sees us – with the potential to be beautiful.

Father, thank You for making all things beautiful in Your time. Thank You that I am a new creation in Christ.

101
Obey or Die

Read: Genesis 3:1-7
Key verse: You will not eat from it or touch it, or you will die.

Wood ducks build their nests in the hollow of a tree as high as sixty feet from the ground. The mother duck doesn't begin incubation until all the eggs are layed, which means the eggs all hatch at approximately the same time. A few days before the babies hatch, they make faint peeping sounds, and the mother communicates back to them. The babies are familiar with her voice even before they hatch.

Now comes the hard part: usually within twenty-four hours of the babies hatching, the mother will leave the nest, drop to the ground beneath the nest and call to her babies. The babies must obey and jump immediately, because the mother quickly leads them to the safety of water. If a baby doesn't jump, it will starve to death. If it waits a while, the mother and other babies will have left the area. Failing to obey leads to certain death.

God told Adam and Eve they would die if they did not obey. Their choice to disobey introduced sin and death to mankind, and every person born on earth will sin and eventually die a physical death. But we, too, have a choice. We are doomed to eternal separation from God, not because we were born into Adam's fall, but because we *choose* to remain there. God graciously gives us the opportunity to live with Him forever by obeying one simple command: Believe in the Lord Jesus Christ! And we can't put that decision off indefinitely. The Bible says *now* is the day of salvation (2 Cor. 6:2).

❖ Make the decision simply to accept Christ.

I want to obey You, Lord. Thank You for loving me enough to die for me.

102
Freed from Traps

Read: Psalm 124

Key verse: Our soul has escaped as a bird out of the snare of the trapper.

For centuries, birds have been trapped and killed for a variety of reasons. The snowy egret and the common egret have beautiful plumes that were in great demand for ladies' hats a hundred years ago. Hundreds of thousands of bird skins, including herons, parrots, birds of paradise, and others flowed through the centers of the millinery trade – London, Paris, New York. But even in the North American wilderness, trumpeter swans were caught for their meat as well as their skins and quills. Trumpeter down made the best quilts and feather beds.

In the time of Shakespeare, larks were considered a delicacy. But they were too small to be hunted with guns or arrows available at the time, so nets were used to trap the birds. The nets were set out on the ground before daybreak, and the larks were enmeshed when they came down to feed.

In today's scripture, David reminded the people of Israel how God had been on their side and helped them escape from their enemies. David concluded his song with the declaration, "Our help is in the name of the Lord." We need to claim this defense against the nets in our culture today. We can become enmeshed in the evils of addictions – not only to drugs and alcohol, but to gambling, pornography, immorality, and violence on television. Even seemingly harmless things like sports and computers can keep us from using our time and talents for God.

The good news is we can be freed from the traps into which we walk. The same God who rescued Israel will save us if we repent, admit our need for help, and turn to Him.

❖ If you are in a trap, admit it to yourself and then to God.

Father, I want to be free. Your strong name is my help. Out of my bondage, I come to You.

103
Compasses

Read: Psalm 119:93-105
Key verse: Your word is a lamp to my feet and a light to my path.

Probably no facet of nature has baffled more people than the incredible migrations of birds. How does a bird set and stay on an appropriate course? What guides the bird so perfectly that it can return thousands of miles to the same backyard it left six months earlier? Physicists offer all kinds of theories about forces in the environment, such as thermal radiation (hot and cold air flowing upward), and orientations based on the earth's rotation. Astronomers think birds use stars or the sun as beacons. Other scientists suggest birds follow visible features such as coastlines and rivers. Of course, all these cues would be useless unless the bird were equipped with sense organs capable of reacting to them. The bottom line? We still don't know all the answers.

One thing we do know for certain, however, is we human beings have a compass to show us the way to God and how we should act along the way. The Bible, our compass, tells us everything we need to know. Everything God's Word does for us is explained in Psalm 119, and Jesus assures us in the New Testament that the Holy Spirit will guide us unto all the truth (John 16:13). With our compass and our guide, we never need be lost. Scientists still don't know how birds migrate, but God does!

❖ Pause when geese fly overhead, and take a moment to praise God for His omniscience – He knows everything.

Holy Spirit, lead me to know and speak the truth.

104
God's Jewel on Wings

Read: Genesis 1:26-31

Key verse: God saw all that He had made, and behold, it was very good.

If the grandeur of the eagle, the beauty of a cardinal, or the joyous song of a wood thrush do not inspire us to worship God, surely the miracle of a tiny hummingbird would cause us to marvel. The smallest of all birds, it is truly a fantastic flying machine. With wings beating eighty times a second, this jewel on wings can fly backwards and sideways, and can even hover like a helicopter. It can also burst into speeds of sixty miles per hour.

One of the most striking features of hummingbirds is their iridescent plumage, especially the heads and throats of adult males. The way these iridescent feathers are structured has to do with wavelengths of light and precise positioning, so the bright flash of color will be seen only when the bird is directly facing the observer. The different colors of iridescence in other kinds of hummingbirds are caused by tiny variations in the thickness of microscopic discs and air bubbles in the feathers. How easy it is for us to casually observe the hummers at our feeders, and never wonder at how truly amazing these tiny bundles of energy are. The hummingbird surely must have made God smile when He created it.

The Bible tells us in the very first book that He was pleased with His creation – everything was perfect, exactly what He wanted. Throughout the book of Psalms, we are reminded of God's awesome power and glory – His name is excellent, and all His works are meant to praise Him. And in the last book of the Bible, Revelation, John declares God is worthy to be praised, to receive glory and honor, for by His will all things were created – even the little hummingbird.

❖ Take time today to marvel at one of the creations God designed to delight you: a flower, a butterfly, a hummingbird.

Oh Lord, our Lord, how majestic is Your name in all the earth!

105
The Freedom of Eagles

Read: John 8:31-38
Key verse: If the Son makes you free, you will be free indeed.

In flight or at rest, the bald eagle is majestic, with his white head and tail lending dignity to his imposing appearance. The bald eagle was chosen as the symbol for our country long before the United States had proven itself to be a great nation. Chosen because of its long life, great strength, and regal appearance, the eagle also represents freedom – living on tops of mountains fearlessly, coming and going at will.

The concept of freedom was perhaps more precious to our Founding Fathers than it is to us. They knew they would have to fight and die for the freedoms we take for granted today.

In today's scripture reading, Jesus explains true freedom is found only in Him and He had to die to get that freedom for us. When we are slaves to sin, we are not free. People who do not recognize Jesus as their personal Savior cannot know the inner freedom that comes when we know we are completely forgiven. Those the Son sets free are free indeed!

❖ Sing a patriotic song today.

Thank You, Lord, for our country and for all those who have given their lives to keep it strong and free.

End Notes

Devotional 2: *Prayers from the Ark* by Carmen DeGasztold, translated by Rumer Godden, The Viking Press, 1962

Devotional 3: *Owl Moon* by Jane Yolen. Philomel Books, 1987

Devotional 22: "Feathers Are Letters", *Something Special* by Beatrice Schenk de Regniers, 1958

Devotional 29: "Something Told the Wild Geese", *Poems by Rachel Field*, Macmillan Publishing Co., 1934

Devotional 43: *The Story About Ping* by Marjorie Flack and Kurt Wiese, Viking Press, 1933

Devotional 65: *The Runaway Bunny* by Margaret Wise Brown, Harper & Row, 1942

Devotional 70: *Crow Boy* by Taro Yashima, Viking Press, 1955

Devotional 76: "Your Cheatin' Chickadee Heart," *The News Journal*, Wilmington, DE, May 3, 2002

Devotional 88: *Inch by Inch* by Leo Lionni, Scholastic, Inc., 1994

NOTES

NOTES

NOTES

NOTES

Pleasant Word

Printed in the United States
201003BV00001B/184-246/A